PRAISE FOR
Doing Time With Charlie

YWAM is known for an amazing diversity of ministries because we help people to listen to and obey the voice of the Lord and then we try to encourage them in their new ministry. When you read the story of Kay Page, you will be like me, saying *"Wow!"* I had never heard of someone being led by God to do what she's done, but I've seen that a burden has now been laid on her heart to do what most Christians would shy away from—become involved in prison ministries. If you want your world rocked, read this book.

> Loren Cunningham, founder, Youth With a Mission;
> author, *Is That Really You, God?*

Doing Time With Charlie is a love story. Kay and Charlie—a prisoner serving a life sentence in a maximum security prison in Maine—are both Christians, and they approach their relationship with honesty but fear. Although they encounter great difficulties and face rejection, they do not give up but pray constantly.

The book is full of pathos. There is sadness but victorious faith. This is a story of redemption, Charlie's as well as Kay's. A riveting story and good reading for all.

> Tom Phillips, retired chairman and chief executive of the
> Ratheon Company; the man who led Chuck Colson to the Lord

In today's times, it is important to know that, in the most extreme situations, people find each other and share their lives in ways that exemplify peace, kindness, and redemption. *Doing Time With Charlie* tells that tale in a way that inspires, and shows that in the most unfortunate circumstances, one can find inspiration and healing.

> Lyn Levy, founder and executive director, Span, Inc.
> (providing services for prisoners and former inmates since 1976)

In her memoir, *Doing Time With Charlie*, Kay Page takes us behind a lot of walls. Initially as ignorant as most of us are about what prison life entails, Kay corresponds with, befriends, and eventually commits her life to a man who, after being arrested for a serious crime, has also been arrested by a life-changing faith.

We see behind the walls both Kay and Charlie have erected in their lives to deal with hurt, guilt, and dashed hope. We see the work they do to surmount those walls. With disarming honesty, Kay tells her story, the story of her unlikely romance, of her journey toward healing and wholeness, and of her unflagging commitment to loving Charlie and honoring her God. Doing time with Kay's book will challenge and hearten you. You'll come to see that walls are no barrier to life, love, and faith.

Susan Zelie, writer

DOING TIME WITH CHARLIE

DOING TIME
WITH
CHARLIE

Kay Page

KAY PAGE

Deep River
B O O K S

Doing Time With Charlie
© 2013 Kay Page

All rights reserved. No part of this book may be reproduced or transmitted in any form or by any means, electronic or mechanical, including photocopying and recording, or by any information storage and retrieval system, without permission in writing from the publisher.

Unless otherwise indicated, all Scripture quotations are from the Holy Bible, King James Version. Public domain.

Scripture taken from the NEW AMERICAN STANDARD BIBLE®, copyright © 1960, 1962, 1963, 1968, 1971, 1972, 1973, 1975, 1977, 1995 by The Lockman Foundation. Used by permission.

Scripture quotations marked NIV are taken from the Holy Bible, NEW INTERNATIONAL VERSION® NIV Copyright © 1973, 1978, 1984, 2011 by Biblica, Inc.® Used by permission. All right reserved worldwide.

Published by
Deep River Books
Sisters, Oregon
www.deepriverbooks.com
This book is published in association with The Benchmark Group, Nashville, TN. benchmarkgroup1@aol.com

ISBN-13:9781937756956
ISBN-10:1937756955

Library of Congress: 2013945541

Printed in the USA

Cover design by Joe Bailen, Contajus Design

"Remember the prisoners, as though in prison with them, and those who are ill-treated, since you yourselves also are in the body."

Hebrews 13:3, New American Standard Bible

"Lord, please convince those in authority in Maine's prison system to reconsider the deeper value of the Law; give them courage to exercise mercy and an understanding that without mercy, the Law becomes criminal…"

FROM A PRAYER BY VAUGHN SHEPHERD OF CANADA

Dedicated to all the men and women in the United States
who are currently incarcerated, on parole, or
on probation, and their families.
God be with you all.

Although this is a true story, some names and events have been
changed for the sake of privacy.

Contents

ACKNOWLEDGMENTS

I see clearly how authors have a hard time noting all the people who went into the writing and publishing of a book. Does one note all the people in their life from birth until the book gets published? All have gone into our experience in a nonfiction book. So here, I attempt to list just some of those who have helped on this book.

First, my dear husband Charlie was my chief coach and cheerleader on this. He not only wrote parts of the book but also read all of the chapters before our last spring together and critiqued it for accuracy.

My children and their spouses and grandchildren were supportive of us in so many different ways. I love you all, including my stepsons. Bless you.

Patti and the Writer's Group—for all the years of listening and helping out in every way. Could not have done it without you. Do you have it memorized yet?

My friends and support team, thanks for getting me through the good times and especially the tough ones. You know who you are.

River of Life Church and all its many in-and-out people have encouraged me and listened to my pleas about those inside the walls. I am grateful to all of you. And many people who did time happened into our place of worship and stayed. I hope you all feel a part of this project too.

Sandi and Scott wrote when they heard of my marriage and said, "That sounds like a story." And then proceeded to lead and encourage all along the way. The friends who were there to support me as I got to know Charlie are too numerous to mention. Many of them are under pseudonyms in the book itself.

To Patti, my agent, who believed this book would get noticed. Thanks for the support and encouragement.

All my friends in YWAM have blessed me along this path. Your non-judgmental ways are awesome.

To all the team at Deep River, thanks for the support and encouragement to get the project to completion under unusual circumstances. Rachel and Kit, you are gems.

Finally, to everyone who prayed me through all sorts of circumstances to get our story into print: I could not have done it without each one of your prayers and deep caring. Your names should all be published, but due to the nature of the subject of my book, I have chosen to use pseudonyms for almost all the people in it. Ray and Pat, along with Matt, are real names, and they have walked with Charlie and me through each and every step.

Thank you one and all.

Chapter 1
PRISON LETTERS

W ant to write to a guy in prison?" My friend's question caught me by surprise, but it shouldn't have. Lacey and I had just watched a video of her husband Bill's funeral, and through our tears we were talking about Bill's great passion, helping men in prison. A good cry helped clear the air, and we were ready to go on.

Sitting in their home, I still couldn't wrap my mind around the thought that Bill had died. I still expected him to come back from work or shout from the TV room. This man who had helped me start to walk out of my own dark victim prison, who taught me to begin to love and trust again and what it means to be a Christian, had been so quickly taken from us. His death to cancer three months before had left a big empty place in my heart. I could only imagine the loss and pain that Lacey was feeling. And how about all those men in prison to whom Bill had been a lifeline?

Without another thought I said, "Sure, I'll be glad to write."

At the table where we had shared many meals, Lacey and I sat down to talk about quite a few possibilities of inmates I could write to.

Okay, Lord. To whom do you want me to send a letter?

Charles Page was the name I thought the Lord was highlighting. Hmmm. One small name.

"So who did you pick?" asked Lacey after I was pretty sure I had one the Lord was underlining.

"Charles Page," I said, writing it down on a scrap of paper from my pocket.

"Charles Page? Charlie Page! I can't believe you picked Charlie Page! He is so well-known in prison."

Lacey's animated response made me wonder what kind of man I'd chosen. Was that my heart beating a little fear?

Father, did You really say to choose this man? Is he going to be trouble?

Lacey looked as if I had opened a box I shouldn't touch. I sensed an unusual anticipation from her.

"Charlie is one of the leaders of the Christian inmates at Maine State Prison. He's been in there for twenty something years and he's a faithful follower of Jesus. A long time ago he met the Lord at Kairos." Kairos, as I knew, was a Christian weekend intended to introduce inmates to Christ. Lacey gave me the prison address, then stood up and scurried off into the kitchen. She returned with plates to set the table for supper, a pot roast that was filling the house with its delicious fragrance.

"Bill used to say Charlie is respected by both the guards and the inmates. You could write to him if you want."

I put the pieces together, curious about this man I was choosing to write. *This Charlie is a well-known person in prison. And Bill admired him.* That was all I knew. *But what in the world is a well-known person in prison anyway? Lord, does that mean he is dangerous or a leader?*

As we ate together, Lacey continued. "But Kay, there is another guy who needs you. He is really young. He needs the positive influence of a Christian woman," she said as she handed me another name with the same general address at the prison. She wanted me to have an encouraging experience for my first attempt at being a prison pen pal.

I left Lacey's house that windy, wet fall day in 2002 with two names and two addresses. The next morning my two small, neat white envelopes went out in the mail, with little expectation that anything would result from this venture. My best hope was that a pen pal relationship with someone in prison might open a new doorway for ministry in my church. Ten years after becoming active in missions work, that was my new job: getting people excited about missions at home. My background was such that I loved reaching out to people in trouble. So would others, I reasoned.

My brothers had tormented me when I was very young and then into my teens. I was shaken by my father as he sang songs to me about being fat. I learned not to stand up to him or my brothers or the taunts got longer. I am sure all of them thought it was just in fun, but my tentative steps into the world around me were successfully thwarted. Perhaps the strongest feelings of inadequacy came from my struggle with weight. I was well aware of being ten pounds over the norm when I was in junior high. No one bothered to tell me that was not a lot, so I turned to eating to calm myself. The cycle of gaining and losing weight was deeply ingrained by the time I was in high school. Other aspects of my life were emotionally unhealthy as well. When I was a teen and having a meltdown, my mother had no idea how to handle me other than to tell me how shameful my crying was. So for the long years between seventeen and thirty-two, I learned never to cry in front of people.

During college in Boston, I got involved in the civil rights movement. I entered the culture of black people and their plight in the US. Next thing I knew I had joined SCLC (the Southern Christian Leadership Conference—Dr. King's organization) in Boston, and a friend in college helped me to raise funds for a march. I left school for a week to join the finish of the march on Montgomery from Selma, Alabama. Not at all a proper thing for a girl to do at the time.

It was also during this era that free love was becoming acceptable. I helped someone who was in the civil rights movement with me get an abortion. Later, while I was working in another state, a fellow teacher asked me if I knew how to get an abortion. It was still illegal, but I got the information for her. We talked, and I comforted her as she left for Mexico.

After weathering life through college, I was a perfect candidate for an abusive marriage. The father of my children was a man I met at a party and eventually married. In this marriage it was easier not to stand up for myself. After all, if I did, I would be overpowered by this man. Still, more than half a lifetime ago I joined Alanon, a group for wives and families of alcoholics. That was perhaps my first step into walking away from being a victim as I was able to share with people who understood the awful thoughts and fears of living with a troublesome person. Five children came from our union, and they are a joy to this day. The Lord walked me to the place of finally saying, "No, I will not take any more abuse, physical or verbal." But I still had a long path to recovery.

Once again single, I got a job teaching in a little country schoolhouse to support our family in the late seventies. At the same time, the greatest change of my life took place: a good friend who taught in the same school system as me asked if I wanted to go on a retreat called Cursillo, where I would learn about Christianity in a very real way. Experiencing unconditional love on this four-day retreat brought me quickly to tears. I wept buckets and felt the love of God overwhelm me as the shame started to melt away. I was now following the Lord.

Desiring to continue with these Jesus lovers, I joined a prayer meeting and there met Bill and Lacey. Perhaps Bill saw my hunger for more of the Lord, and he took care to see that I was paired with women who would help me walk through deliverance from the fears that had held me captive for so many years.

Shortly after I found the prayer group, my mentor began to instruct me clearly, with simplicity and mostly by example. Bill lived what he taught. People in my prayer group accepted me with no strings attached. Overpowered by love, my life turned around. The Bible had answers where I did not even have questions yet, pouring life into me as I read. This was contrary to the teaching I had received as a child that the Bible was just a book of legends and myths. God became as real to me as the freckles on my hand.

God's relationship with me was a love story as I learned to seek His voice each day. After attending the prayer meeting for a while, I joined a group of ladies called the "praying over." Each of the other women had wonderful spiritual reasons why they had come. I went because it sounded like a good way to have a break from being housebound. I told the ladies that. We laugh now, but we learned through practice about hearing from God.

For five years I was a part of this group, praying for our little prayer community. We met every Monday, really helping us to grow close to God. We were not better than others or smarter or anything, just willing. More often than not we were learning to love others and sometimes failing miserably. Just as in any relationship, as the years went on I grew in knowledge and understanding of God. After a severe grease burn one night at our Friday night prayer group, two friends prayed with me for the pain to go. It left almost as soon as my friends put their hands on me. I still marvel over that more than thirty years later. Physical healing was real.

When it came to majorly emotional times, both Bill and his wife were there to support me. That was a breakthrough in itself: I didn't mind if they heard me cry. It was the first time ever I had felt that a man was trustworthy enough to hear my tears. Bill listened right along with Lacey. Many a night he would say things like, "Kay, you don't need that in your life," pointing out how a bad relationship with some man was getting me upset over nothing.

As I continued growing in relationship with Jesus, my life continued to change. Emotional scars from years of abuse left me. Often a change would come when I least expected it. One day I was forced to face the rage that had hold of me. As I walked in the house after the car would not start, one of my kids said, "Get out of the kitchen. Mom is getting mad." I was shocked and realized my daughter was right. I was about to erupt like a volcano. At the time, it was normal for me to foolishly scream at the car or, even worse, at the kids, when I faced what I saw as impossible problems. Not even aware of how much anger had affected my life and family, I was taken aback. And God took my rage and showed me better ways to handle anger.

Financial solutions came in abundance. At one point I had saved enough money in my envelope budget system to buy a washing machine to replace my old wringer washer that was dumping water on our plywood kitchen floor. A little bit each month was put toward the washer, and finally there was a big amount. One hundred and fifty dollars had been put away, surely more than enough. Off the kids and I went to Sanford in our little car, and we stopped at what I later found was the most expensive appliance store in town. With five kids trailing me, I looked at the washers. On the way to town one child had said, "Can we get a dryer too?" So I got bolder, looking also at the dryers.

"Can I help you?" asked a pleasant salesperson.

"I wonder if you have a floor model or something that is not as expensive as this one." I was pointing to a washer that was priced very high by itself, even without a dryer.

"Hey, Joe, we have any floor models or damaged washers? Lady wants a deal," he yelled back to someone.

"No," the man in the back replied, "but my wife wants to sell our washer and dryer. She is tired of white and wants a yellow set."

I asked, "How much?"

"How much, Joe?"

"One-fifty," came the reply. I had my washer and dryer. And they could deliver it to me for free because the seller worked in an appliance store. God was showing me how exact He can be.

At work, another passion captured me—teaching others to read well. Not all the children in my class were learning to read, and my friend Nanda and I agonized over this. She suggested we pray for an answer, and lo and behold, we got one. Slowly we came up with ideas for doing this task well, and *all* the kids began to read. Now I had an outreach, and it was a fine outreach indeed. For years after I worked to try to get good reading practices into Maine schools. People came for miles to get help with reading and teaching reading.

Twelve years after coming to know God, I was happily growing in my relationship with Jesus while attending a church in New Hampshire. I was still teaching at the little country schoolhouse. Each day I would get up before school and write in a prayer journal. My children were on strict orders not to get up early. Step by step the Lord was embracing me more, and I went deeper.

One morning at prayer time I wrote down something very different. "You will be going to countries all over the world and working in schools with street kids." *Ha, this can't be You, Lord,* I responded. I had never been past Chicago. The very idea was frightening to me. *I am teaching and doing well training others to use what I have learned about teaching reading. I teach homeschoolers. I can help kids to read who have never learned. I have even taught adults who are older than me.* That day I needed to get to school early because I had traded bus duty with Judy, a coworker, so that I could go hear the head of Youth with a Mission (YWAM) speak in New Hampshire. My daughter Camelia was with YWAM and had invited me to come, and my pastor would be there as well.

Forgetting what I had written, I left school that day with relief and anticipation. What a joy it would be to see my daughter. She was the missionary in my family. The words I had written that morning were gone from my memory as I enjoyed the ride over to the mission base through the lovely woods of New England. After a scrumptious dinner at the base, we settled in to a tiny hall of sorts to hear from Loren Cunningham. His talk was quite inspiring—until he got to the part about schools. My hearing had been off for many years already, and I wore hearing aids.

"What is he talking about, schools?" I asked my daughter. She was well trained in translating for me what others were saying.

"Oh, he's talking about DTS." I was familiar with Discipleship Training Schools–they were the course by which my daughter had gained entry into YWAM. Agitated by her explanation, I could not hear a word that was spoken for the rest of the time. I kept thinking I had recently heard something about me and schools around the world.

"Okay, I am going over to talk to Loren," I told her as soon as there was a break. I just could not go another step without asking him what he had meant.

"Hi, my name is Kay. I was wondering what you meant when you said schools all over the world tonight?"

"Oh. Elementary schools," he said, and I rudely turned away, trying to hide my embarrassing tears. I could not remember just when I had written down that I would be going all over the world and working with street kids because the day had been so long, but I knew it involved elementary schools.

"What do you do when the Lord tells you something very scary?" I sobbed to my pastor, who was right behind me in line to speak to Loren.

"Probably talk to your pastor," he answered. We met soon after that to go over what I thought I had heard from the Lord.

Over the next three years the Lord taught me to wait for His timing. At one point I felt the Lord say to go to the nearest church to my house in Maine. Of course I argued. In Maine I would be at a church where I did not know many people. But the Lord graciously delayed my joining Youth With a Mission as I built relationships at home.

Soon I was preparing to go to missions training through a YWAM DTS. But there remained one last assignment to teach reading while at home. A student from Afghanistan came to me because the schools had not taught him to read. He was nineteen and very bright. His foot had been shot off in the war with the Soviet Union, and he had come to New Hampshire to have his leg cared for. Our lively times of study at my house after school one day a week were exciting. I loved getting to know someone from a completely different culture. I can still see him laughing as he tossed off his prosthesis to chase my kids, hopping on his good leg.

Now, ten years after joining YWAM, I had just mailed two letters to two men in a Maine prison. I began to think about the implications. To be honest, some of my first thoughts about Charlie were that he might be dangerous. What did I know about this man? What does anyone know about prisoners? Lacey had spoken well of him, and I knew she would not deliberately set me in a perilous situation. But he could be a sociopath for all I knew. I had seen TV shows about prisoners, all scary.

A week later, I got back a letter from the young man I had written, which I opened quickly. I had never received a letter from a prisoner. It was stamped with the now familiar, "This letter is forwarded from the Maine State Prison-Warren. The contents have not been evaluated and the Maine State Prison is not responsible for the substance or content of the enclosed communication." Sadly, this young man was not at all interested in talking about Jesus.

Shortly after, I received a letter from Charlie. I am not sure what I expected. Perhaps threats or improper invitations. Or at least a good con job about needing money.

Instead, I received this:

Dear Kay,

It was good to receive your letter. I was surprised. I was glad to hear you know Bill, and that he is special to you. He also was a father to me while he was alive. I miss him too.

I am locked up for count now, so thought I would write. I hate count. They make us do it five times a day and I have other better things to do. But that is life in prison.

Well, things are pretty boring here, but I have a job in the wood shop. I love carving loons—big ones and small ones. They are then sold at the Prison Store.

I met the Lord at a Kairos weekend, and He changed my life. I am so thankful for Him every day.

The rest of the letter was full of stories about how the Lord was working in his life as well as polite questions about my life. Okay, I thought. No drama here. I could write to this man. So I did.

He responded to my next letter with more about the Lord, but he also began sharing details of his past. He described himself as "a simple country boy," and though we had led very different lives, we found many common experiences related to marital pain, anger, and more importantly, the love of Jesus in our lives.

As more and more letters came, I was surprised to learn that Charlie was a very humble man, one who talked a lot about Jesus, and one who was repentant for his crime. I did not sense he was saying that to get on my good side. He would write simple things like, "I pray every day for the families I hurt as well as those others in town who were hurt. I wish I could take it back, what I did. But I did it and have to take the consequences." I could hear his pain and his honesty.

Without my knowing it, I had embarked on a relationship that would once again change my life.

Chapter 2

LETTERS AS MISSION

Jesus was all I'd thought I might have in common with those men inside the walls. What little I was learning so far about Charlie surprised me.

After a career as a teacher and then as a foreign missionary, I was now working full-time as head of missions at River of Life Fellowship, my home church in Sanford, Maine. Sanford aspires to be a city, but it's more like a village, spreading out from a grassy town square where people still gather to walk and talk local politics. At Christmas one can still find a crèche in the square. A church bell that strikes out on the hour several times a day makes one think of a simpler age.

I had settled in this area while surviving a stormy divorce, raising five kids, and serving as a public school teacher. After my children were mostly on their own, I joined Youth With A Mission as expected and worked first in the College of Education in Hawaii and then went off to Iraq, Bosnia, and Kosovo. I could have chosen easier places, but as a survivor myself, I wanted to bring healing and endurance skills to kids whose lives had been shattered by war and injustice.

Shortly before my encounter with prisoners, I had received visa papers to go to Afghanistan—still another war zone—but my team had dissolved. My pastor, Ray Noyes, met with me afterward to discuss what my next step should be.

Ray is a very down-to-earth person, and he and his wife, Pat, are good friends of mine to this day. Ray has a fire for God and a ready, open heart to all he meets. The day we first met, he gave me a word from the Lord about going into missions. It was not long before I was coming home from many war-torn places able only to weep for the kids there. Each Sunday as we came into the presence of the Lord, I would be unable to do anything but cry.

I remember one Sunday in particular, around 1995. As soon as the presence of the Lord seemed strong, I began crying again. I was sitting up back, trying not to be noticeable. Ray announced, "Don't pay any attention to Kay. She just came back from one of those war countries, and she cries a lot when she comes home."

Another time I was wearing an outfit that an Iraqi woman would wear to a wedding. I was about to share a little about the country and my experiences with the people. Long before sequined clothing was popular in American culture, there I was sitting in church with a full floor-length kelly-green sequined dress with sleeves that could only be described as wings when I spread my arms. I also had a matching kelly-green headdress. The outfit more or less stood out among the other communicants, who were mostly in jeans and T-shirts—more typical dress for our services. I noticed that Ray kept looking at me. Finally he burst into laughter and said, "I can't keep from laughing any longer. That weird lady up back in a bright green dress is coming to talk to you now." A merry introduction was made, and soon the whole place was laughing with us as I walked to the front.

Still another time I remember him telling the congregation, "Kay is back. She was in one of the 'stans.' I can't remember which one. Kurdistan or Kyrgyzstan. Kazakhstan? They are all stans." Ray is not a person who pretends to be perfect. He is full of fun, tempered with extreme kindness.

As we sat down to lunch to talk about my options in 2002, he wanted me to consider staying here instead of trying another tactic to go to Afghanistan.

"Kay," he said, "I would like you to pray about staying here in Maine for now and only going on mission trips for short periods."

"Okay, but why?" I asked.

"I think the time has come for you to focus on getting others in church to see that we are all missionaries. They still don't get it."

In the ensuing year, I looked for ways to help our people see the need for local and international outreach. I began writing Charlie at that time. One of our first teams went to Dearborn, Michigan, to work in a program for recent immigrants, people who had come to the US to better their lives. After a major prayer initiative for my town, I bought a house in a poor neighborhood. I dreamed of fixing up the garage and having it become a hangout for kids. I wrote about it to Charlie.

Another obvious mission possibility was reaching out to people in prisons in ways other than in letters, but I still knew little about how to do that. Thanks to Bill and Lacey, I had begun to view people inside the walls as needy human beings just like me. Though I still had my share of prejudices about prisons and convicts, I was starting to see that Charlie's life amounted to more than the crime that had gotten him inside. If I could write letters to these men, I was sure others in the church would write letters too.

"I was married twice before," Charlie wrote. "I have two boys." Later he continued, "I was married the second time when I got arrested." He freely admitted to making a mess of his two marriages. I admired him for taking responsibility for what he had done. I began to talk about places where I had to take responsibility for my part in my failed marriage.

I shared with him about my marriage and my willingness to manipulate so I always looked like the good guy. Tentatively I wrote, "Charlie, I was abused also. I learned to stand up to that by calling the cops to report assault and battery. But it took years before I stood up that much."

Charlie talked more about his situation. He alluded a few times to abuse in his background but said, "Almost everyone in here has been abused in some way." And he started calling me a scrapper. When I protested, he said he admired scrappers. I realized he meant that he admired those who did not cower. God must be changing that area of my life too.

For all the differences in our growing up, we had arrived at similar conclusions. We valued honesty, we took risks for our beliefs, and we both expressed that we liked simple living.

"I am a very honest man; I hate playing games," Charlie wrote. "Almost everyone in here is innocent. But I am guilty." I remember feeling relief at his honesty. Many people in my life had not been able to achieve such openness.

I worked hard at being truthful, and I didn't like playing games in friendships, but I had done it. I had tried to manipulate men for my protection. Admitting that was a first step toward change. In my early life, I had been intimidated and hurt by men saying and doing inappropriate things to me. My usual defense was flirting. I did not flirt to win the heart of a man, but to control the interaction and shield myself. If I charmed a man enough he would like me and not hurt me—or so my theory went. My challenge now was to write letters in friendship, without any game playing. Each letter back to Charlie was carefully and prayerfully crafted. They were friendly but not flirtatious and contained basic information about my family and my work in missions.

Knowing the Bible says to visit those in prison, I tacked onto the end of one letter, "Do you want me to visit you or call you sometime?" With no idea as to what someone in prison would talk about in person, I felt this was something I should ask him even though it frightened me. I was determined to find something in Maine that would be a good mission field, and people in difficulty had always fascinated me. I had worked in a juvenile prison teaching reading, but this was different. Charlie was an adult and adults really scared me, more so because he was about my age. But they must like getting calls, I reasoned. I was busy creating an "us and them" mentality, and I did not even recognize it.

In a week or so he wrote back, "I don't like calls and don't do visits."

Okay. That was fine with me. The Maine State Prison is in Warren, a good two-and-a-half-hour drive over long, lonely highways. I didn't want to make such a long drive anyway. I had no particular interest in visiting prisoners. And in addition to that, I was hearing impaired and didn't like calls either.

With this defensive attitude, my prejudices came out. Men in prison deserve to be there. Men in prison are dangerous. Men in prison will never change. With Charlie's letters and some honest reflection, I realized these prejudices sprang partly from my long-held perception of men. Yes, men were intimidating; they deserved to be manipulated; and they never changed. I knew deep down that was not universally true because the Lord had used some godly men to deeply influence my life. But those prejudicial thoughts kept resurfacing.

In my first letter, I had mentioned to Charlie that Bill was my spiritual father. I had no doubt that Bill had shown the Father heart of God to Charlie and other inmates—many of whom had been brutally abused themselves. Bill's unconditional, healing love had rocked my world. It exposed and undermined my prejudices about men. And it opened my heart and mind to the redemptive, healing grace of Jesus. Bill's love for people in prison had also given me a glimpse of their humanity. I knew he'd be pleased that I was now in a budding friendship with someone inside. But I still wasn't ready to trust this man Charlie.

During my missions training, I had worked hard to overcome my attitudes related to men. I didn't want any of that negativity to slip into my letters to Charlie. So I had to write and rewrite letters again and again. As I wrote about my life, I gained more insight into the roots of my long-held beliefs. Raised in Massachusetts—in a white, middle-class suburb—and as a true child of the 1960s, I had rebelled against social mores and the duplicity I saw in my own home. This rebelliousness and disrespect for authority (particularly men in authority) was rooted in rejection and had affected my life more than I had realized.

One day as I read more about Charlie's life now and work carving animals in the wood shop, a new thought occurred to me: a person in prison could be radically changed. In theory I knew this was true, because Jesus was changing me. However, I had not applied that truth to this person in prison. Here I was writing to this man who was in prison for life, and he seemed very nice, relatable, even godly. A changed man?

The Lord was showing me that much of what I believed about prisons and people incarcerated there had been formed by TV, movies, and other images from the media. The Bible gives quite a different picture. Many of the Bible's key figures—Joseph, Moses, David, Paul—were prisoners or criminals at one time. Soon I knew the battle for redemption of my mind in this area had begun in earnest.

"You know," I told a friend, "I missed so much of what the Bible says about prisons and prisoners. So many people who are Bible heroes also were in prison." I had read again and again the verse about visiting those in prison as if they were Jesus. And Charlie held Paul as his hero.

Our letters started in the fall of 2002. By spring they were a nice exchange of news about our respective jobs and what God was doing in our lives. Charlie was becoming a friend who happened to live far away rather than an inmate who lived in prison. Charlie asked me about where I lived and if I would help him if he ever got out of prison. I wrote back, "Yes, of course. I will be your hands and feet on the outside." This was no longer a project to me; Charlie Page was a person, and I enjoyed our correspondence.

"Yes, of course I know all the rock 'n' roll songs. 'Rock Around the Clock.' 'Jailhouse Rock.' All the stuff from the 1950s," Charlie wrote in answer to my question. That response touched me because I loved the music of my teen years.

Generally, he wrote in the morning while he waited for his "house," as he called his cell, to be opened for head count. "A few days ago I was looking out the window of my room into the back field. I saw about seven turkeys. I also saw a big buck and three does. I love the woods. Jesus has truly blessed me."

Road rage was my typical reaction to the wild turkeys I came across on the back roads of Maine. They were in my way. Now I was embarrassed at my thanklessness whenever I thought about Charlie, grateful to God for the simplest things in his restricted world.

Soon I found myself eager for his letters to arrive. In dreary conditions, this man walked out what Jesus had said—content in all circumstances. I knew Charlie was teaching me—that Jesus in him behind the walls was teaching me.

"Charlie, you are always so appreciative of the animals you see through the window," I let him know.

"I was not always this grateful," he admitted. "I arrived here a very angry man." He often told stories of his life on the street, which included many fights. "I wanted to pound a guy who did this or that all the time. I was a fist fighter. Didn't know yet that was not the way to stand up to someone."

Another time he said, "It took me five years of being here on a life sentence before I could accept that I was really here for the rest of my life. Once I accepted it, I had to learn to just deal with today. There is not a single thing I can do about my past or my crime. It is gone. I cannot undo it. And there is not a single thing I can do about tomorrow except to live today making right choices."

His words were a challenge to me. *Help me understand, Lord, how someone does this. Help me understand how I can do this.* That letter was probably the first time I realized I was learning deeper things of the Lord from him, in a mutual trust and exchange between a brother and sister in the Lord.

The risk of exposing my heart to Charlie, a man, seemed worth it now. I was growing because of our friendship, and it was becoming more important to me than I could admit. I pressed forward, praying like crazy. Apparently I was writing a radical follower of Jesus, who did what the Lord said to do as best he could. Often his simple question to me as I spouted the latest "Christian" theory, was, "Where does it say that in the Bible?"

"I don't know," I would reply. "Isn't this what it means?"

As we wrote about various issues, I became more careful to search the Bible before writing to Charlie on a subject. He had taken a whole course on the New Testament and the Old Testament. He loved discussing the Bible. He repeatedly challenged me to study the Scriptures to see what they really said.

As I learned about life in prison, I became aware of how much I had missed about the Lord's concern for those in prison. Jesus started His ministry at the temple by saying He had come to set the prisoners free. He chose to end His time on earth by dying with two criminals on a cross. Just before that, Jesus was put in prison Himself. The pain and loneliness people inside felt was something I had never considered, but Jesus certainly had. Now I found myself praying for Charlie and praising God for the many satisfying and pleasant exchanges we'd had in our letters.

Pleasant, until one day he wrote, "Kay, ask me anything you want. I will try to answer it." I had already asked him lots of questions. Tons of them. The next week he said the same thing.

"Ask whatever you want. I don't mind any questions." He repeated this message in several letters. Why was he writing this?

Suddenly it occurred to me that he wanted me to ask what his crime was. That was the one thing I did *not* want to know. Dread came to me even thinking the question. How could I ever ask that of someone who was inside a high-security prison? As long as we were just talking about Jesus, I was fine. But "What did you do to get life in prison?" That was another story altogether.

Why is Charlie doing this, Lord? I don't want to ask him what his crime was. I really don't want to know. I'm afraid that if his crime is what I think it is, I will not be able to write anymore.

I couldn't trust what my feelings would be if he told me he had committed a murder or some other heinous crime. I wanted to just encourage him, not to deal with the full reality of his life—or my own. But here he was teaching me to deal with just that.

I had started out writing to Charlie because of Lacey's request, then it became a kind of missions project. But what was it now? How deep should I go? I knew the Lord would have His way.

Okay, Lord, I will ask. Might as well get it over with.

"Charlie, what was your crime?" slipped into my next letter. I fretted and prayed earnestly, almost hourly, until his answer came back. I knew he was an honest man. He would tell me the truth. Yes, I was expecting murder, but I desperately wanted his crime to be something else. What else would get you a life sentence in Maine?

Charlie's next letter dropped like death in my mail slot, and I prayed once more before opening it.

It was murder.

Chapter 3
CONNECTIONS OF THE HEART

My reaction? Not what I anticipated at all. Instead of my being laid waste by the news of Charlie's crime, the Lord reminded me of my own sin.

Kay, you helped commit murder when you helped your two friends get abortions. You felt so bad that they had gotten caught having sex outside marriage that this seemed the lesser of two evils—to help someone get an abortion. You were concerned with getting caught, not with the child coming. And it was illegal at the time.

Abortion had seemed much less of an offense than murder in the sexual revolution of the mid-1960s. But when I got the letter from Charlie, the Lord brought into the light just how much this wrong thinking had crept into my spiritual walk. Certainly I had repented of the two abortions, but there was a nagging voice in my heart still saying that somehow abortion was not as bad as the murder of an adult. God was about to correct that thinking.

Thankfully, the Lord had already begun to turn me around. He had given me a great love for children and a new sense of how they are valued by God. As I taught school and raised my own children, I came to clearly see so much about children in God's eyes. When trying to establish better relationships with parents, it dawned on me that parents are the original teachers of children. I was overwhelmed with that one day, and during my next parent-teacher conference, concerning a kid who needed help behaving, I used this revelation. I told the mother, "You are the best teacher of your son. I would like to hear what you think about this. I have a lot of experience with kids who misbehave and can help some. But you have to tell me what you think would help." God's whole view of family and children was so perfect, but I had denied the concept of children as people. Now, God was again showing me that He will use every detail of our lives to expand our revelation of Him.

Ironically, ten years after that first encounter with abortion, I had found myself confronting the issue from an even closer perspective. Close to the expected birth of my fifth child, I needed help. I sought assistance from a social service agency.

"What can I do for you?" the social worker asked.

"You know I am having a baby, and I live out in the woods," I replied, knowing she could figure the twenty-five miles I had to drive to get to the hospital to give birth.

"I know you have other children. How many?"

"I have four, and I am not sure I can drive to the hospital and get the kids to a sitter after I know I am in labor." I explained that my husband was not in the picture.

"Kay, you really don't want to have that baby, do you?" Her voice trailed off as if it were not really a question. Abortion was now legal. Did I want it?

"Uh," I answered, stunned. Somehow I urged my feet to get up, and I walked out the door. In helping friends in the 1960s, I had felt numb. Now I knew the reality of children and that the child inside me was a person. I was enraged by this lady asking me to get rid of my child, but also knew vaguely that in my past I had thought the same way.

Back then, I began the journey to repentance. In my new Jesus-centered worldview, abortion was murder, just like Charlie's crime. I had helped two friends cross the border of Mexico to have abortions with much forethought. Charlie had no forethought in his crime. He mentioned in his letter that he had taken a "handful" of prescription drugs and was hallucinating when he committed his crime.

Now, sitting there in my comfortable living room, with sunlight shining through my windows, I wondered why I was out of prison and he was inside. He had already spent years in prison for his crime. I was living free and easy. The full impact of what I had done fiercely pounded me as I read Charlie's letter with deepened understanding. I did not deserve this comfortable life. After rereading his words a few more times, and doing my best to repent again, I knew I had to respond quickly and truthfully.

"Charlie, I did the same thing. I helped two people get abortions."

I cannot remember anything else I said to him in that letter, but in becoming friends with Charlie, I had to look at all my prejudices about murder and look closely at my own crime. Pride had blocked my healing for many years. Today I would be honest just as he was. Again, I was learning from Charlie.

Charlie's reply came from his heart. "No one on the outside has ever said anything like that to me," he wrote. Charlie knew that abortion, hate, and murder were the same sin in God's eyes. It was just that he had never had anyone from the outside say it to him. "You know you are forgiven," he offered.

With that, my dreadful admission became a powerful bridge for our friendship. Sheer honesty about my covert crime helped me understand this man and him understand me. Sharing with him was a milestone for me and a great relief.

"Funny," I mused to a friend one day. "We on the outside do not imagine that someone inside can minister to us. Somehow it is supposed to be the other way around. At first it seemed strange to have Charlie counsel me, but I found I was looking forward to his response to any admission of sin in my life. I realized he had seen just about everything while there in prison. All my seemingly shocking admissions don't put him off one bit."

Through our letters, I felt layers of pride and self-deception being stripped away. Perhaps this is what happens in all deep friendships, but I had never experienced this in any previous friendship, especially not with a man. The enormity of the sin in my life would have overwhelmed me before. Now was the Lord's appointed time for my healing, and Charlie walked with me through all the feelings that I poured out on paper.

"Charlie," I wrote, "I am sinking in the reality of the abortions I helped. I am so upset."

"Now that is done," he answered. "You are forgiven. It is gone from His mind." This time I received that forgiveness *because* I had finally understood the depth of evil in my heart. Why had I run from truth and explained away my sin for so long? For the first time in years, I felt complete freedom. Like Jesus, Charlie had looked at me first and not at my past sins. Not many outside do that with the childlikeness he showed me.

Lord, you are doing something wonderful here.

As time moved on, our letter writing increased and our friendship deepened with each exchange. Writing to Charlie was awakening something deep inside me. How I admired this man!

Shortly before I began writing Charlie, I'd had two formative experiences with men as I was working in missions. One was a very wrong relationship with a non-Christian. I had entered into it with full knowledge that it would not work. Friends counseled me against it, but I pursued it anyway. The relationship quickly soured, and I was deeply grateful for the support and prayers of faithful friends.

Then I jumped into a friendship with a Christian man. He was a good and funny man. He and I enjoyed being together and had lots of laughs. We had a lot in common, but I sensed he was not God's best for me. It was almost as if the Lord was saying I could be in a relationship with him if I wanted—I could choose. I talked to my brother about an e-mail I had received from this man. I did not like something he had said and wondered what I should do about it. My brother reminded me that I had never been totally honest with my ex-husband.

"Ted, I don't know what to do about this guy. He keeps telling me how to be careful. I am not afraid of most things, and I am careful," I said. "It's patronizing."

"Tell him the truth. Tell him you don't like it. Kay, you have been so eager to please men that you become no longer yourself. Do you want to go through that again?"

"No, not at all."

I wrote back and told this man why I did not appreciate what he had said. I really worked at being polite and not hurting him—just pointing out how his attitude was making me less of a person. I was sure he was not aware of this. He meant no harm. But two e-mails later, the friendship was gone. Losing him did not hurt much because I now knew I did not want a friendship with a man who was condescending to me, or with one who could not talk openly about a relationship.

Many men my age were like that. Our generation never shared about relationships. I had learned in my YWAM training to share openly and politely if you thought there was some kind of relationship starting. I was grateful that in that last friendship, we had gotten to the problems early and that I now had the beginnings of a friendship that was open. What a contrast between this man and Charlie, who was impeccably honest and also a risk taker.

One day, my friend Nanda and I settled down to a quick lunch in town during one of my breaks from renovating my new home in the drug neighborhood. I had been bubbling about the people I was meeting and also about my letters to Charlie. She could see what was happening and decided it was time to challenge me about it.

"Nanda, I am not in love with him," I said. "I haven't even met this man!"

"You are enjoying his letters an awful lot," she refuted.

"Yes, I am. I'm also discovering some new things about myself because of him."

Earlier in my journey toward healing, I had recognized that I liked the otherliness of men. They are formed by God to think and act differently than women. This was a huge revelation for me, and it was nice to admit it. I had always liked being around men even though I had been hurt by some. With Charlie, I was deliberately becoming vulnerable, sharing bit by bit some of my past.

"Nanda, you know I want to find someone to grow old with, but that someone could not be a man in prison," I said. She just smiled, and I found myself talking to the Lord about it.

Father, help me find the way forward in this friendship. You know me and can make clear who You want for me if she is right. You will have to show me what I am feeling for Charlie.

With the two experiences before writing Charlie, I had decided that God did not have someone for me. The choice to walk out living alone for the rest of my life was better than being in a marriage not of God. So writing Charlie and enjoying his letters was not love, I decided. Passion was easy to get into. Now I desperately wanted friendship, only friendship. And I was learning how to have just that.

It wasn't easy, even though it was enriching. The whole conversation with Charlie about murder was scarier to me than anything I'd experienced in Iraq or Bosnia or Kosovo. I'd once had an assault rifle pointed at my forehead, but that was nothing compared to this irrational fear of being honest with men.

Letters to and from Charlie were bursting with prayer and dialogue about our walk with the Lord. Infatuation never happened. A mature, respectful, sincere, and deepening alliance became ours. And I had yet to enter the walls. What bondage fear had caused me! And what freedom I felt now! God was changing me, and I was gaining confidence that I could have genuine affection for a man. Affection. Where did that come from?

Chapter 4

FIRST TIME INSIDE

As our letter writing increased, I was constantly humbled by Charlie's simple faith. My thoughts about my own problems were often, *Lord, get me out of this.* On the other hand, Charlie just wanted the company of Jesus through difficult situations. Charlie's constant plea was, *Lord, walk me through it.*

When a fight broke out in Charlie's pod (the prison area where he lived), he would often tell what had happened in his next letter. Every fight was potentially dangerous, but his take on each serious incident was usually, "The Lord was walking me through it."

He also faced chronic health issues, connected with diabetes. Outside prison, we choose our medical facilities, doctors, food, and people who minister to us in prayer. Charlie's desperate medical needs were being met by a small, understaffed infirmary. He wasn't one to complain. "After all, this is a prison," he wrote.

Because of diabetes, Charlie needed to regulate his diet and medications. But prison did not always include good food. Through the years, he had depended on the Lord for his health. "God knows the day I am going to die," he would tell me after some painful incident in his legs due to diabetes. I knew that he was not in control of the day he would die, and he really kept that in the Lord's hands. Again I was learning from his simple approach to disease and dying.

I began to probe a bit more about how he had come to faith in Christ. "I went to Kairos, and it changed my life," he wrote. "I grew up in the Catholic Church. I knew God was real, but I only went to Him if there was an emergency. I did not know about God's love. But on the weekend I learned about that love. I was flooded with the love that came through the staff on the weekend or through just prayer." Wow, we had more in common. I had met the Lord through a very similar weekend retreat.

Having no hope of full and final forgiveness for murder, Charlie had walked in overwhelming guilt during most of his years in prison.

"On that weekend I really felt God's forgiveness for the murder. Other guys were feeling it too. Then this guy on the outside team shared that he was guilty of manslaughter. He knew he was forgiven. God really does forgive all the sins. All of them."

With so many years inside, Charlie had felt that only those inside would speak of murder in their past. Charlie was touched by the confession of manslaughter. Having so many outside people come into the prison to love on prisoners really made him see God's love in action.

"Me too, in a way," I wrote back. "I attended a Cursillo around twenty-five years ago," I shot back in my next letter. Cursillo and Kairos share the same roots and follow a similar four-day format, which is a short course in Christianity. Kairos was our common culture, the place where we met on the same ground. As I attended Cursillo, many people around me had just loved me in numerous ways. They had opened up their hearts and lives in a real way, sharing sins from their past, and the Lord had several talk to me who'd had abortions. They had been forgiven. I was snowed under that they would actually share this.

That weekend was also the first time I had ever shared openly about sleeping with my ex-husband before we were married. And I had never thought that anyone else, especially these together ladies on the retreat, had done such a thing. Turned out many shared that with me. We then walked through a forgiveness ceremony, and I truly felt God's love overpower me in a very real way. I met the Lord.

"We really do have a lot in common," I wrote.

"I am seeing that," he replied.

Since we had each come to know the Lord through this four-day weekend ministry, we were anticipating the prison's next Kairos weekend in the spring of 2003. During the event, I planned to work in the church kitchen outside, and he would pray for speakers inside before they gave their talks. Charlie and I were hoping others would experience the love of the Lord through this weekend.

I shared in letters with him what the preparation for Kairos was like for the outside people. He told me about preparation activities on the inside. Six months before the Kairos weekend, men and women from the outside start meeting to plan, pray, and prepare for the event. The people who were to go inside had to have security clearance, so early on I filled out forms required by the prison administration. I would work outside but go in for the final event.

Topics for a Kairos weekend include the nature and character of God, repentance and forgiveness, and the freedom that comes from living in Christ. Volunteers participate in an overnight retreat before the actual time with the inmates. This time helps to build relationships between the people from the outside who will be leading the Kairos weekend. God invented relationships. Every aspect of the final program with the men is discussed, and the main theme is always, "Listen, listen. Love, love."

The closing ceremony that spring would be my first trip inside Charlie's prison, an adult prison. "Charlie," I wrote, "I will be there at the closing." I had decided I really wanted to participate in the final ceremony because Charlie and I had both come to the Lord at such an event. I wanted to experience it.

"I'll be inside, waiting to see you. I will be sitting across the room from you, and I will wave," Charlie wrote. Then he added, "They won't let us shake hands anymore, but that's okay."

This became my first disagreement with prison authorities, and I had not even entered the facility. I wanted to greet Charlie personally, but I knew he and the other inmates would not be allowed to mix with the Kairos kitchen volunteers. So I decided to overlook my disagreement with rules. At least I would get a visual.

I sent Charlie my passport photo so he would know who to look for. I figured the red hair on an older woman would identify me. I could not imagine how I would know him. Oh well.

By now I had looked forward to "going inside" for months, but my first time inside proved more unsettling than expected. Not because it was dangerous. Purses were left locked in our cars. The prison rules dictated what we could wear and how we must act. No jewelry except a cross and wedding rings; no denim because that was what the inmates wore. No this, no that. The list seemed unending. Most importantly, we could not go near the inmates.

After a tiring weekend of work at the church outside, we headed up to the prison to attend the closing. Upon arrival, I signed the logbook, which keeps a record of all volunteers inside the complex. Surrendering my driver's license (for identification) and my liberty for a day seemed a small price to pay to attend what others had said was an extraordinarily wonderful event. And I was excited to finally be able to see this friendly man I had been writing. We had shared by letter, very gradually, more and more of our lives. So far he was not abusive or pompous. And now we would see each other, albeit from afar.

Arriving at the front lobby of the prison, Lacey and I sat down to wait for our call to go inside where Kairos would be. She said it would be in the gym. Before leaving the lobby to go inside, Lacey had me go over once to meet a local politician, my representative, John Tuttle from Sanford. He was there to attend the Kairos. He did not live far from either of us. Lacey said he really listened to his people.

Lacey and I walked through metal detectors just once. Experience with airport detectors helped me. Others in our group went through a few times trying to figure out what caused the beep. For them next came the pat-down search. Once, while on a mission trip in Turkey, I had gone through a surprise internal search. That incident had taught me to be prepared for the worst. Nothing like that happened here.

However, nothing prepared me for the finality of that chilling clank of doors closing me off from the outside world. I was inside the walls now. The giant doors had rhythmically closed at the command of a button pushed. Steel against steel. In the silence of the walkway, the door closing was like the heavy thud of a train rear-ending an eighteen-wheeler. We were *sealed in*. The stark reality of being shut off from the outside world in a high-security prison was a finality I could not have imagined.

Two guards called rovers walked both before and behind all of us as we traveled inside to reach the gym where the closing would take place.

Each time we entered a different part of the complex and walked through a sally port or door, we heard, "Stop. We are going to count you." And they did.

Along the way, we could see inmates through glass, but they did not come near us. Their stares and reactions told the story of longing for human contact. Some were visible down the hall from the sally ports. Seeing women, I suppose, was what stopped them in their tracks to look. Maybe they had heard that a lot of outsiders were coming. But there they were, lined up by the glass doors, leaning toward us. We were another set of glass doors away, and still they stared. There were others who were trying to be cool and not look while they were looking. Still others were grinning and waving openly. I liked that honesty. I waved a tiny wave so as not to concern the escort officers. The mom in me wanted to reach out to these hurting guys, to wrap my arms around them. Surely they could use a motherly or fatherly hug, but our instructions were clear. No contact with anyone in prison blues. It was not going to happen.

Abruptly we were there, in a huge gymnasium, with only a few guards. There were bleachers on the left side of the room. The team men from the outside whom we had fed all weekend were seated on folding chairs in the middle. Signs and banners with Christian themes were displayed all around. A band seated in the front was tuning up for some kind of musical presentation for us. And of course there was the usual shriek of microphones being placed on a stage of sorts under high gymnasium ceilings.

Our chairs were across the room. Following the rovers to the right side of the gym opposite the bleachers, I gratefully settled into a chair to rest and soak in the surroundings. As I looked about, taking in the large room with basketball hoops and other sparse gym equipment, my mind could not help wandering to the anticipated event of meeting Charlie. The certainty of soon being in the same room with him was unsettling, but I felt the anticipation of finally seeing what he really looked like. After all the outside guests were settled in, inmates who had previously attended a Kairos weekend were escorted through the door and told to sit on the bleachers across from us. *Which one is Charlie?* I silently wondered.

The scene reminded me of a high school graduation, except for the sight of guards milling about. Lacey began pointing out inmates she knew and telling me what she remembered of their walks with the Lord. When she caught someone's eye, he would wave to her. She never mentioned Charlie, and I was not going to ask. I was *not* in love by any means!

One fellow was Lacey's pen pal who wrote her often. He wore funny red suspenders, and his laughter with his friends indicated the suspenders matched his personality. Other inmates were signaling Lacey and laughing. Another lady was using the hand sign for "I love you" to an inmate who seemed to know her. Lacey said the inmates called her the cookie lady.

These expressions revealed bonds of friendship that could not be contained by all the "hands off" and "stay apart" orders. I began sensing the joyful and familiar presence of the Holy Spirit. Most of the inmates going through the weekend for the first time had no idea what would be waiting for them in the gym. Our anticipation jumped another level when horns started playing "When the Saints Come Marching In." As the door opened and the men came in, my heart just leapt with joy.

We all stood spontaneously to welcome these precious guests who had passed the test and stayed with the activities until this final celebration, the closing. Tears filled my eyes as I considered the significance of what had just happened to these new children of God. They had fought their way to forgiveness. They had experienced God's resurrection power. They had met Jesus.

Loud horns played, and we sang our hearts out with the men as they entered, our new brothers in Christ. I am sure we would have danced as unto the Lord like David of old if the instructions to us were not so specific to stay put by our chairs.

The guests themselves looked quite bewildered as they saw friends from prison on the bleachers, their teachers in the midsection with chairs, and last of all us, the strangers seated off to their right. They finally responded with shy and shining smiles as if they had recovered their thoughts. Other than staff members, some men had probably not seen any outsider, especially women, for years. After a pause to take it all in, the men entering really caught the joy of being with "family" from the outside.

"Brothers, we introduce to you your brothers and sisters in Christ," someone announced with aplomb.

The change that God makes in people always astounds me, but it was the unexpectedness of the setting that most affected me. I now was openly weeping for joy.

After the reality of having outside people in the room with them settled with the men, everyone calmed down for the program. As planned, dignitaries were introduced, speakers were heard, and finally the men who had participated in the Kairos weekend got up to speak. One after the other told of their transformation during the few days here.

These men were the stars of the day. One young man got up and shared how lonely he had been all his ten years in prison. He did not look as if he was old enough to have been there ten years. His loneliness was broken. Another older gentleman shocked me with a story of being inside forty years. *How could someone do that?* I wondered. He shared how full of anger and the desire for revenge he had been. It seems he just did not care anymore until he felt the love of God flow.

Those of us who were from outside the walls were humbled by the realization that God is in the business of changing people. Crying, laughter, and overwhelming joy abounded. Our hearts were beating with every word, so in love with our new brothers were we. After seeing what God had done with the men, I understood a lot more about my friend Charlie. His radical change from his past had catalyzed at Kairos, just as mine had started on a similar weekend twenty-five years before this.

Even the guards noticed the change in the men. I overheard one talking about the transformation to an incredulous friend. "I have seen this each time I have been working on a Kairos closing," he explained.

Honored and humbled to be part of this team, I felt the experience confirm what I knew already—that God is real and that He changes us as He heals us. I felt privileged to be near men who had decided to alter their lives at such peril. After all, to talk of following Jesus in our state's highest security prison was in itself a danger. But then, these men were risk takers in the first place. Perhaps this would be the first risk to bring hope and goodness into their lives.

The day was incredible. But it held one major disappointment. Lacey said Charlie was not there.

Chapter 5

FINALLY

S o much anticipation. So much disappointment. Did Charlie not want to meet me after all?

As I drove home from the Kairos weekend, my mind flooded with questions. Was Charlie afraid to come because of me? Was there some crisis in his life? Was he sick? There was no way to know, so I prayed and hoped and wondered. The Kairos weekend had radiated unimaginable joy, but I came home feeling a touch of sorrow.

My attention turned to my next scheduled trip to Kosovo, still over a year away. I wanted someone to go with me for a short-term trip. River of Life, my home church, had a vision to help some needy Kosovars, and I had picked a poor Roma family to receive our attention.

The conflict in Kosovo in 1999 erupted over ethnic differences between Serbs and Albanians. The Roma, also known as Gypsies, were another racial group and intensely disliked by both the Serbs and Albanians in Kosovo. They were the lowest rung in Kosovo's social pecking order. Our adopted family had ten children, all living in a one-room shack built with cardboard walls over a skeleton of two-by-fours and covered by an old blue tarp. When I first met this family, I helped Evan, the father, get some food. Though we didn't speak the same language, his weather-beaten face and toothless smile conveyed how much he appreciated the help for his wife and children.

Many times since meeting them, I had been the humble recipient of a cup of chai and some store-bought cookies available for the equivalent of five cents a package from this desperately poor family. All ten children and their mother were summoned to come and sit with me in the hovel. Seating me always as the guest of honor, they gave me a place on the mattress facing the door so I could see who was entering their simple home. This is the place of protection in Kosovar culture. If armed men entered, I would be able to escape faster by seeing them first.

Prior to the Kairos weekend, my friend Carrie Sue had organized prayer and raised money for Kosovo and this family. She kept track of the family's needs in order to have supplies and cash to buy food for them when I left again. All this planning was a magnificent diversion for me as I waited for another letter from Charlie.

Four days after the weekend, a letter arrived. I thought he would say so if he had not wanted to meet me yet. It had dawned on me how much I wanted to meet him. I opened the letter slowly, prayerfully, because my fear of rejection was fierce. This might be my last. I considered that he was overwhelmed by the prospect of seeing me in person. Not so!

"Kay," the letter said, "I felt so bad that I could not meet you. I really tried to get there. The pain in my leg was so strong I felt like I could not breathe. I missed being one of the prayer people there for the weekend. Maybe we will meet at the next Kairos weekend."

Even as relief swept over me, I immediately felt concerned for his welfare. My sister has Type 1 diabetes, so I knew some of the problems but not in much depth. Charlie's letters showed me just how painful and debilitating this infirmity could be.

At church the next week I announced, "Anyone who is interested in helping people in prison, see me. I went to an amazing ceremony for people who met the Lord. If you want to come, you will attend an amazing work of God. Let me know if you want to sign up to help at Kairos in six months."

After the church meeting, some gathered around me to ask about Kairos. I told them, "This is where this fellow I am writing met the Lord. He is in for murder, and he is totally a new person."

"Have you met him yet?" someone asked.

"No, but he usually attends. He was quite sick that last time. We will see him in the fall."

"What does he have?"

"Diabetes," I said.

"Wow, they make him stay in prison with diabetes?" This person seemed quite surprised. I had never thought about it. For me, the strange question epitomized the lack of thought we put into what being in prison involves. But Charlie was becoming part of our little church now. People were beginning to see him as a person, not a prisoner.

I also understood now why Bill was so animated every time he talked about Kairos. "Men walked to the podium weeping," I penned to Charlie, "each knowing his own crime and receiving forgiveness for his sins after years of believing his sins were unforgivable." Amazing. "Waves of love flooded through the gym, and I heard of incredible changes in men who had been incarcerated for years." Now I was the animated one, seeking to share by mail the things I had seen. I was raring to go to another Kairos to see the ongoing miracles of changed lives.

"I know all that goes on. They come back to the pods excited. I am glad you got to see it all," he wrote. Charlie liked to remember his own Kairos in the 1990s as he listened to men in subsequent closings.

One curiosity came to mind. Years before Bill had said, "Kay, this one man committed murder, but the Lord brought him to his knees. He is a great big guy. Weeping and broken before the Lord." Bill had never mentioned Charlie's name. Charlie told me he stood six foot three. That fit "big." I wondered if Charlie was the man Bill had told me about.

When Charlie had written earlier that he did not want visits, he had said, "You bring the outside in." An odd term. "You would remind me of all I am missing outside," he had explained. "I spent five years just deciding that I would never get out of this place, and I don't want to go through that again. I have nothing against you."

As the fall of 2003 and the next Kairos weekend approached, my heart was wrestling with the ever-looming thought, *Charlie really may not want to come to Kairos because I bring in the outside.* Kairos also brought other outside people into his world, a bittersweet reminder of what he was missing by being locked up for life. If he made it to the closing ceremony, it would be an added bonus for me on an already blessed weekend. I did not want him to not attend Kairos just because I would be there. So practicing my new skill of being honest with a man, I asked him.

"Oh no. I would not skip it because you are there. Go ahead and come in." So I would.

Bill must have been laughing in heaven as he looked down on my cautious attempts to pursue relationship with this man by mail. Maybe he knew Charlie and I would make good friends.

Charlie loved hearing about my plans to go to Kosovo. The danger of serving in a war-ravaged country prompted him to pray for my safety and success in the mission. As the Kairos fall event neared, I was praying too—for the twenty-four men who would be opening their lives to Christ that weekend, inmates who had never attended a retreat. I was going to work in the church kitchen near the retreat, making meals for the men teaching. I would attend the closing ceremony once more. "Finally we will see each other," Charlie said in his last letter before the retreat.

Truthfully, I wanted to see what he looked like. He was my friend. He lived with continuous pain in his legs, but he didn't complain. From our letter writing, I suspected that he might miss Kairos for medical reasons. The worsening pain in his legs often kept him from going to church and work.

Your anticipation is suspiciously high, I told myself. Carrie Sue and I talked and then prayed, asking the Lord to guard my heart, especially if I did meet Charlie. Given my track record with men, I didn't want another infatuation.

"Well, it is good to be back," I told Lacey as we arrived at the church where we would sleep and work while the men were at the prison. When the men got back from the first Kairos meeting, they shared some exciting stories. They also invited us to pray with them for some men who obviously did not want to be at the retreat.

Charlie had written once, "I never wanted to go to my weekend. I went because I thought it would shut up Matt, the chaplain." The chaplain had been praying and asking for Charlie to attend, and Charlie was forever grateful for that. I imagine the chaplain prayed a lot for him, and God answered.

After the cleanup of the church on the last day, all of us who were working in the kitchen went to the prison. Past the razor wire and through that mammoth bulletproof door again, we would see the wonder of the Lord's love manifest in twenty-four men. After some last-minute instructions as to what to do and say, where to walk in the gymnasium, and where to go after the Kairos closing, we moved into the cavernous interior of the prison.

The walls were still as stark, cold, and drab as before. Guards were as businesslike as at the first closing I had attended. Probably due to some security precaution, they did not respond to a simple smile. Handed a panic alarm to set off if we were in danger, we were now fully equipped for our trek inside. Actually, one of my biggest concerns was setting off the panic alarm by mistake; that would be just like me. *I would rather face the danger, but rules are rules,* I thought. I clipped it to the pocket on my slacks.

On our walk toward the gym, our escorts stopped often to count us. It would have been comical if it had not been so real for Charlie's life, taking "two steps forward and one step to count." Unexpectedly I understood what Charlie meant when he gave the impression in his letters that count time was a frustrating day-to-day ritual. It interrupted other important tasks for him. I could not imagine this five times a day, day in and day out for the rest of my life. Even as that thought crossed my mind, I could almost see his words in a letter saying, "Oh well, that's life in a prison." I could walk out the door at the end of the day. He couldn't. The constant regulation of the simple task of walking from one place to another might seem overboard to me, but Charlie had to accept it as part of life under high security.

Another reflection that filled my head as we walked through to our destination was the cost these Kairos inmates had to pay to walk out their faith. Being in prison and following Jesus takes guts. Charlie had once written that one prison creed is "intimidate before someone intimidates you." A man who decides to follow Jesus is sometimes considered weak. To stand up to the intimidation that will conceivably increase with the decision to pursue Jesus, a man must be strong and sure of Jesus's might and power. Soon the room would be filled with the brave men who had decided to walk that path.

Walking to the gym and sitting, we began to look around. The tension rose as we awaited the new lives coming to meet us. Finally, a hush and a pause.

The guests of the weekend were filing in. The room erupted into wild cheering, hooting, and hollering. The exultation of the Holy Spirit filled the room, and my heart soared, anticipating the events still to come.

During the ceremony, Lacey whispered to me more stories as various men told of their moment of love and salvation. These were not quiet, hang-back men, but tough guys, bad boys, grown and transformed into men of God. Like us, they had to stay in their assigned seats. We all were told to keep quiet during the program, but a lot of hand signals using American signing were shooting back and forth. The sign of "I love you" passed from the inmates through thin air to the Kairos kitchen staff so often that it actually seemed noisy.

Peace washed over us, almost like a warm spring rain, and it was not because of the "be quiet" rules. The Lord was present, silently filling the room like a pillar of fire, commanding our attention.

"There's Charlie," Lacey whispered. *Stay cool,* I told myself, immediately on alert for a new reason. "He's the tall one in the back row of bleachers, with white hair and a beard." I looked up there and spotted him. *Oh, he is tall. I like tall. Cute beard.* Somehow I had to hide that I was sneaking another peek, trying to see Charlie's face.

One hurdle over, I turned my heart and mind back on the emerging stories.

Charlie Speaks

Well, now, this was not just any meeting. It was the first time for me to meet my new lady friend, who I had been writing to for quite a while. Over a year now. I was especially looking forward to this Kairos weekend. The Kairos outsiders talk about life and things we all need to do to make life better—a life with God in it. If inmates would let God walk them through things, life would be better for all concerned.

On the last day of Kairos, certain inmates give speeches about what Kairos has done for them. At the closing, I planned to meet Kay for the first time. I had never seen her except through a picture. I knew it would be a very special time for me and for her.

We were coming to the end of the evening, and the guards were taking the outside people away. I was looking for a redheaded woman as I stood on the bleachers. I could not see her, but I knew she was there. When I saw Kay, I started walking toward her. At the same time, she saw me and started toward me. I was sure it was her. I pointed my finger at her and stood on one leg. She did the same. Picture that in your mind, and you are doing pretty well.

As I look back, it was rather funny. Two grown people standing on one foot and pointing at each other must have been quite a sight. We looked like two long-legged whooping cranes getting ready to mate.

That's when I heard one of the guards yelling at me. She was telling me not to go any farther. So I took another step. She told me again I had to move back. But I stepped out a little farther. She started toward me to make sure I did not move anymore, but I did. I finally stopped to listen to what Kay was saying, but I couldn't understand. Too much noise. Nor could she hear me.

So our first "meeting" was all smiles and gestures. Prison authorities forbid us from mixing with outsiders because they are afraid that contraband will be passed between us. This could happen. It has before and will again. I understand why there is a rule, but I do not have to like it.

As Kay left through the gym door, I realized that we were never even able to shake hands. We did not talk, even for a minute. She was there and she was gone that fast. But we would have a chance to meet again, because I had decided to make it happen.

Kay Speaks Again

Once more, I was struck by the adventure God had in store for me when I will go and do as He leads. During my times of service in war-torn countries, I've had such awesome experiences with the Lord. As I would sit and marvel at the Lord's doings, I would wish I had a video of what happened. It would be so fierce and heartrending, and I wanted to share it with those who had sent me out. Not possible.

I had decided that precious times like these were just for me to hide in my heart, or in this case, Charlie and me. They could not be recorded for others. Though I was surrounded by guards, inmates, and Kairos workers, I felt I had a moment to treasure with Charlie, being "alone" in the same room with him.

The Kairos closing ceremony fairly chimed out the love and pleasure of the Lord just as it had the spring before. Somehow elation seems greater when deeply savored within the walls of prison. To see people come to know the love of Jesus Christ just never gets ordinary. He touches hearts every time.

Many men who came from devastating circumstances, who had committed serious crimes, stepped nervously to the podium to speak with tears falling and worship in their hearts. For perhaps the first time since they entered the walls, they showed emotion other than anger and hate. Realizing they were loved—no matter what they had done— brought light to their faces. They were safe.

One thing was bothering me, though. When Charlie and I met, I had felt more than friendship. *Lord, it is hard to die to this flirtation. How ridiculous. He was way across the room.* My heart was not obeying my orders, and I was no longer sure I wanted my heart to be stone toward this man. Somehow my plan to not be in love was falling apart.

Chapter 6

Visiting in Prison

Soon after the Kairos weekend in the fall of 2003, I received a long letter from Charlie. This letter was especially intriguing because toward the end, he wrote, "By the way, if you want to visit me on a weekend, I would like that very much. I enclosed the paperwork you need to fill out." A visitor application form was tucked inside the envelope.

Because of his no-calls-or-visits edict, I had never thought of visiting him; it was a closed subject and a relief. With an invitation now in hand, I found myself agitated and fearful. Why had he brought this up again? Furthermore, why was I so upset?

Lord, help.

Seeing Charlie in a roomful of people or having him on the other end of a letter was okay; going to see him one-on-one was not. I could hardly express to my close friend Nanda the deep-seated concerns his letter triggered in me, complicated emotional stuff from my past relations with men. To be honest, my weight was always a problem. He had seen me now and still wanted me to come, actually saying that he would like that. My experience was that men might want me for physical pleasure or abusive prowess, though obviously that was not going to happen with guards all around. The real struggle was my suspicious heart; what was it he wanted? It had truly never occurred to me he might want to move up a step to meeting in person. Now here was the invite from him.

I doubted his motives but could not figure out his angle. My heart needed to believe that he really wanted a friendship with the otherliness of a woman, the same as I wanted with a man. Was it really that simple? He really liked the thought of me coming to visit because he thought it might be fun?

"That is wild," said Nanda. "The Lord is giving you a friendship with a man in a safe place for you. You cannot get into trouble with him with guards all around."

Nanda had invited me to her home to chat. I could talk about this because no one else could hear. The idea of Charlie and me surrounded by guards struck us both as hilarious. Nanda knew the details of my earlier transgressions with men. She also knew my great effort to stay pure with men, my desire to grow old with a life companion, and the struggle to even believe the Lord would send me someone. She also knew I needed to be honest.

Like me, Nanda was a single mom when we met. We were committed to helping one another grow in the ways of the Lord. As fellow teachers, we spent summers working out solutions to school problems. We had sat for hours at a pond in Shapleigh discussing innovative ways to teach reading, writing, and arithmetic. Could she help me find a solution for how to handle visits with Charlie? She had now been married happily for quite a few years.

"Nanda, I can't have him thinking I want something other than friendship. He does not have other visitors that I know about. What have I gotten myself into?"

"I know. We will figure it out as we go along. He only asked you to come visit."

"Well, my mind is in turmoil. I have come so far in my relationships with men, and I do not want to make another mistake."

"You won't. God will protect you."

We prayed, and I left her house, but my mind kept whirring. After considering the situation for some time, what I felt to be my imprudent side prevailed. Charlie and I were friends, and friends get together at times. It was a go.

I filled out the daunting paperwork, but not without afterthoughts. I almost shoved the letter into the post office box because I did not want to lose my resolve to keep this precious friendship. A saying from my childhood, "Curiosity killed the cat," came to mind. And the childish flip side joined it: "And knowing brought him back."

"Charlie," I said in the next letter, "there is no way I can come on a regular basis, but I filled out the forms. It is such a long trip up. Just so you know."

Another letter said, "I am so busy renovating this house that I don't have a lot of time. I have this new neighborhood where I am living, and I am fixing up The Shed."

"Tiny and I are making a sign for you for The Shed," he said in one of his letters. "We got permission to do it to donate to you. You can pick it up at the Prison Store when we get it done."

Whoa, I thought. So now he is involved with my life at home. Wow. What a thoughtful man. Wow. Keep it cool, Kay.

The Shed was my name for the dream I had for the kids in my new neighborhood. I wanted to serve the kids there and hopefully speak into their lives. We had been calling my garage The Spot, named by some of the teens in my church. They were already getting antsy to work in the hangout and to get to know teens from the neighborhood. In early spring I had left a tiny plastic swimming pool out on my driveway. Someone knocked on my door that summer, and when I answered, a boy around ten asked if he could use the pool on this hot day. He had a friend with him.

"Sure," I said. "Jump in, but I have a rule against you getting hurt, so be careful." I could tell the two boys out there did not know whether or not to take me seriously. But they jumped into the little pool, leaving no room for a third kid. It was quite a sight, the two of them crowding their bodies into the wading pool. I went outside to watch and make sure they were not hurt, and during this time they talked a lot.

"Miss Kay, can we go into your shed sometime?"

"Yes, sometime soon. I am getting a pool table next week. Either of you know how to play pool? I don't." They assured me they knew how and would be there on the Saturday to help set up the pool table when it came. Needless to say, we renamed the garage hangout The Shed.

"You have been approved for visits," Charlie's next letter said. "Call and schedule a day."

Having had enough time to wrestle most of my fears, I called to request a visit. February 21, 2004, worked for me. I was to arrive at 8:30

a.m., which meant leaving home at 6 a.m. I would visit from nine to ten and then return home. No problem. I felt sure I could do one hour without losing control of my life. It would be a long trip for a short visit, but I wanted to go.

"We are going to see each other face-to-face," I wrote, hoping he would be the one to back out. I was going to visit my friend in prison. And I was petrified.

As I read and reread the rules about visiting a prisoner, I nearly drove myself crazy. We could hold hands. He could embrace and kiss the visitor briefly. In former Soviet countries, people embrace and kiss a visitor on both cheeks, even if they are not close friends. Well that was no big thing; he was not Russian. On the other hand, maybe it was a problem. Or maybe I *wished* it would be a problem.

What if he did try kissing me? I was plagued by questions like that. Funny how abuse by men makes you think all men will automatically take advantage of you. As the day approached, I spent lots of time arguing with myself. Finally, like Scarlett O'Hara, I said to myself, "I will think about it tomorrow."

Of course, I already knew the rules about clothing and contraband and kissing. The list said we had to keep our hands visible on the table at all times. That seemed awkward if we were not going to be holding hands.

I sensed from his letters that Charlie was feeling concern too. "What if we do not have enough to talk about? Bring a lot of questions that day," he wrote.

He might be as nervous as I am about this. Maybe we really will have very little conversation.

That thought amused me. I'd never lacked for things to say. And Charlie didn't seem to lack for things to say either. Both of us were older, but I guessed we were both dreadfully apprehensive.

After a fitful night's sleep, I awakened early on the big day. By 6 a.m., I had done all I could do at home. I stuffed the directions I had printed out into my coat pocket and hit the road.

It was the first time I had traveled to Warren alone. The streets I needed to travel were dark and unfamiliar. One stretch of rural highway, lined with dark shadows of trees, extended for miles. I had often wished I could do a painting of the road, the long lonely road. But the roads were mostly peaceful, and my trusty old red Aspire chugged along just fine. This lengthy travel time soon turned into a wonderful time with the Lord. I passed the time singing, praying, and asking for guidance. The bottom line was I really did want to bless Charlie. I wanted to visit him as if he were Jesus. Certainly the Lord had used him to better my life.

When I arrived at the prison parking lot, I shot off one last plea to the Lord for peace. I took a deep breath, grabbed my license, and walked into the now vaguely recognizable front lobby.

Procedures for entering the prison to visit someone were similar to the ones at the Kairos closing, but I had to sign a different book. Following the lead of the other visitors, I managed to sign in without incident.

We had been asked to be there one half-hour before the scheduled visit began. I occupied myself by watching the other visitors, as well as taking in the lay of the room. Sturdy wooden benches filled the place, and people were taking their places along the seats. Some mothers looked more harried than me, trying to keep tabs on little children, who were bored and fidgeting during the long wait.

The lobby was obviously new and seemed rather drab for a new building. The people, including the guard at the lobby desk, acted somewhat tense. Sitting for a half-hour, my own fearsome thoughts seemed to take on a life of their own. From the looks of the crowd waiting with me, I would be walking into a huge room with lots of men. Somewhat comfortingly for me, I could recall what the visiting room looked like from my Kairos weekends. If I remembered right, it had the same institutional look as this lobby. At that time, I had been with people I had come to know during that weekend. At this moment I was not with anyone I knew.

Would Charlie and I have enough to talk about? What if he did not show for the visit? What would it be like to be here all the time and not be able to leave?

Then came more fears about meeting Charlie, pushing on like a roller coaster. Would I even remember what he looked like? Maybe I should not have come. What if I hurt him by not knowing who he was? After all, I had only seen him briefly high up on the bleachers at the closing almost three months ago.

Finally breaking this irksome thought pattern, I heard the signal that we were moving from the lobby to the visit room where Charlie would be waiting. "Visits. No gum, no candy, no cell phones or hooded jackets and sweatshirts," the rover shouted. The "no" list was becoming familiar. *Does Charlie ever hear a yes list?* I wondered.

A rover was assigned to lead us to the visit room, watching our every move. No word would go unheard and no move unnoticed. High security all the way. After passing through the metal detector, we waited in a little crowd for the rover to signal we could move through the cumbersome doors that were now rolling back. We walked silently down an extremely barren hall and entered the sally port, a box about the size of a large elevator with a front and back door. We all crowded in. The first door closed with a loud clang; the door to the visit room opened on the other side into ground zero.

The nanosecond of truth had arrived. Before me was an ocean of faces, men sitting at tables in front of us, mostly smiling, all slicked up, all anticipating a visitor. But they were all dressed in the same blue shirts and dungarees! Panic and agony. They looked identical. Obviously, my mind was running amuck.

Where was Charlie? I'd thought he might be holding up a sign with my name on it, the way people do at big airports in missions. No signs here. I glanced quickly from face to face.

Phew! There was Charlie. He was waving, and a broad smile crossed his face. Relief swept over me from my head to my toes, etching that picture of him in my mind. Why did I think I would miss this big teddy bear with his shock of white hair and a curly white beard to match? I let out my breath and thrust out my hand to greet him as he stood. A good defense is a quick offense.

"Nice to finally meet you in person," he said as we shook hands. It felt stiff and self-conscious. "How was your trip?"

"Fine," I replied. "I made it in good time."

Charlie explained the seating arrangement. "I have to sit in the dark-colored chair. You have to sit opposite me in one of the light-colored ones, not next to me. If you bring someone with you, they could sit opposite and you next to me." Next to him? Where did that come from?

We sat, and he explained the numbers on the table. The rows of tables were all numbered like a bingo card. One, two, three, four, and five in row ABCD or E. Something like that. "If you get here before me, you go up and ask the cop which row and table I will be at while you wait for me to get here. You can sit too," he further explained. "You have to keep your hands on the tables. They are afraid you will be handing me drugs. They used to do that openly in the old prison."

"I read the rules about hands," I said. The height of the table made it hard for short me. Charlie said when they were planning how to build the tables, he had told them it would be too high for most people. "But who listens to prisoners?" My arms were short, making it even more uncomfortable to sit there. But I worked at it.

Praise God, I thought, that I did not have to sit near enough for touch today. Little did I know how much I would hate that rule in the future!

I also had to give Charlie some instructions on my ability to hear. He had to look at me and talk or I would not hear him. His mustache interfered with me seeing his lips. I got him laughing when I asked if he would shave it off for me. It was then I learned that he never used the razors the prison provided anymore because they were such poor quality. He could no longer buy his own. I started to learn just how difficult living in this new facility was compared to the old one at Thomaston where he had begun his sentence.

I cannot recall much of what we talked about at first, but it was a little uncomfortable until we got to talking about Bill.

"Charlie, my father in the Lord was Bill ," I ventured, knowing I was repeating something I had told him in a letter. "He was the one who taught me a lot about Jesus. Funniest thing I remember was him standing on the Bible in the middle of the room, saying, 'We have to stand on the

Word sure as I am standing on it here.' He was very dramatic. That picture still sticks in my mind whenever I am in trouble."

"He was always so funny. Not overly religious. Yes, he was my father in the Lord too. Guess we are really brother and sister," Charlie said with a smile.

In swapping stories about Bill, we found that we both treasured his little sayings, like, "We will be surprised at who we will see in heaven." I would start one, and Charlie would finish it.

"A few years ago I got wrongly involved with a man who was not a Christian. I was in tears about it. My friend Nanda took me to see him and Lacey. I needed prayer. Bill just looked at me and said, 'Kay, Dear, you don't want to do that.' That was all it took. I was in tears, repenting about this terrible situation I had put myself in." We were getting quite personal, more than I had expected. But I trusted him—a new sensation. We had history, albeit by letters.

"Yeah, he could hit the nail on the head faster than anyone I know," said Charlie.

We shared stories of how Bill had constantly pointed us to Jesus no matter how horrible the situation was. Jesus, Jesus, and Jesus.

Bill's death had been a blow to each of us. I shared about how Lacey and I had been friends over the years and how several times we had cried together after Bill died. With this exchange of thoughts, we looked at each other and paused, our first intimate look. My eyes were shiny in recollection, as were Charlie's. Rapidly the subject changed.

"I've been working on the birds, like I told you," he said. "I have twenty-four of them right now. I am carving the heads." He fashioned birds in the wood shop and loved to do wood carving. The twinkle in his eyes grew stronger as he described his work. I spotted a callus on his finger where he must have supported a carving tool, much like I have a pencil callus.

"Won't be long until I get to wood burning all their feathers. I do each line separately," he added. "Each line on each feather. Other places, they paint the feathers. Burned looks better."

Then he asked, "How is the house going?" He was referring to renovations on my little home in Sanford.

"Good, I guess. Lot of work. Sure could use a master carpenter there," I ventured.

"I would love to. I'll ask if I can go to Sanford for a couple of weeks." We both laughed. Good. We were finally breaking down the tension.

After working so hard to communicate honestly in our letters, I could now see the fruit in this first conversation with Charlie. We really did have a friendship. With spoken not written words, we were now expanding our knowledge of each other's lives at an accelerated pace.

I relished the hour with Charlie, and we talked nonstop until hearing, "Visits over." When the guards shout those two words, it is not a suggestion. It's an order to leave. One must move right toward the sally port or be in breach of security. Those two hard words broke up sentences we were speaking, thoughts we were forming, and left questions unanswered.

One hour seemed such a very short time to get to know someone in a context other than letters. We shook hands good-bye with a little more ease than when I arrived, but I did not dare to hug him. On this first encounter, without Charlie saying so, I somehow knew I should leave promptly or risk the guards coming to move me out. I scrambled with the crowd to go home. It was a good visit, but exhausting. And we did have plenty to say.

That week a letter from Charlie came. He thanked me for coming but said that one visit was enough. I was not to come to see him again.

I was a little disappointed—maybe even concerned about the old rejection issues—but I was also relieved. Hard as that visit was for me, I knew it had been harder for Charlie.

The outside coming in.

He felt the relationship would be easier if we went back to our letters. Truth was, both of us were still not ready to come out of hiding totally. I figured he was as concerned as I was about us becoming an item. Neither of us had a good track record; both of us by now realized that a relationship would have to be God's idea.

So the letter exchanges continued with regularity for another two months. During that time, we shared more and more about our lives. Since there would be no more visits, I became bolder in telling Charlie things I liked and disliked. I'd been a chameleon for men all my life, changing my opinions, my hair, my clothing, just about anything rather than disagree with a man. With Charlie, I spoke up if I disagreed. I was becoming even freer.

Much of what I wrote about was beyond anything he was able to experience in his life. In an institution where his every move was regulated, he had so few choices. My letters revealed just how much he was missing. But he didn't stop writing. Now he was involved with my ups and downs, the lack of a full-time carpenter, and the past trips to other countries. It must have been overwhelming, and I was only starting to see what he meant by how hard it was. I had not lived on the inside. He had been on the streets as well as the inside.

It must be so hard for him to just respond politely when I describe all that's happening in my life.

It had been fun to meet Charlie, but my safe place was apart from him. I was quite satisfied with our writing friendship. Maybe I was on overload from having him respond to me with generosity and care, unlike any other man friend I had ever had.

"The Lord is showing me that I should have you back for a visit. I was being selfish to stop the visits," he wrote one day. "In fact, the Lord is urging me to make an effort to have you visit again."

Shocking.

Surprisingly, I was not offended at the statement that he had "to make an effort." Not even one thought about being rejected. This was a miracle. By now I knew that inside, the men trained themselves to appear to feel nothing for another person because they would ultimately be deserted.

I was sincerely moved that Charlie would add the thought that the Lord was urging him to have me visit.

What are You doing, Lord? I don't want to think about that.

Understanding that we lived in different cultures dawned on me. Emotionally, he was also taking a risk. After all, his family had rejected him many years before. It could be another rejection if I said I was coming and never showed. I had grown. Rejection had been a mainstay of my life for as long as I could remember. I realized suddenly that I was being healed of that through our sustained friendship.

Taking a minute to recover from the unexpected change of plans, I quickly set up a time to go see Charlie. It could not hurt, I reasoned. With Charlie saying the Lord had urged him to have another visit, somehow I was not anywhere near as nervous as the first time. I suspected the Lord was trying to show me that this was a really trustworthy friendship. Charlie greeted me at the second visit with a cheery, "Thought you were coming earlier. Didn't I tell you to meet me at the door at 5 a.m. so we could go fishing?"

Over time, there emerged a cadence to our visits. I had planned to come up once every two months, but when he asked me, I came in the next month. When he asked me to come in two weeks, I went. Soon I was coming every week. Yes, Charlie was a delightful man. We enjoyed each other's company immensely, and when the one visit became too short for us, we decided to see each other twice in a day. Thankfully, the visiting times were extended to two hours, a wonderful change. So now I could see him for a total of four hours with only one trip up. We established a rhythm of talking about our lives during the morning visit and praying and reading the Bible together in the afternoon. We truly had a great deal in common. I loved the spirit of this man. His sincerity, his openness, his devotion to the Lord. I loved his laugh too. We laughed and talked about everything. He had a belly laugh. Kind of like Santa Claus.

I also saw that God was using this experience to teach me about prisons. The closer we became during that spring of 2004, the more insights I gained into life behind the walls. I came to realize that if I was to truly know Charlie, I had to face the full knowledge of why he was in prison. I had a label for it, an overall understanding: murder. But I had never learned the full story. That was coming soon.

Chapter 7
PRISON CULTURE

nother window into Charlie's world came from his best friend, Tiny. Charlie had requested that I write to Tiny. As we began our correspondence, I learned more and more about prison culture. I saw common threads between the two men.

Like Charlie, Tiny stands well over six feet tall and has a reputation for being full of fun. And like Charlie, Tiny is a *long-timer,* an obvious reference to his term of incarceration. Charlie noted that lots of friends and family visit Tiny, each one more colorful than the last. I learned that part of prison culture is that visitors become interconnected with other inmates and their visitors. Although they are not allowed to talk to others at tables in the visit room, family and friends of inmates get acquainted while waiting in the lobby of the prison, and friendships are born. I later became friends with Tiny's sister Bette, and we often spoke on the phone or got together on the outside. When Bette passed away in 2009, it was as if I had lost my sister.

Culture contains elements of our history. If I tell you I am Scottish, you instantly know something of my background. If I show you albums of pictures, you know more. If I tell you about my brothers and sister, you know still more. It puts me on the map, so to speak. With little access to the world outside, incarcerated people have developed a unique prison culture complete with customs, protocols, and language. I found that if I respected these protocols and spoke their language, the barriers to communication went down. People inside are understandably cautious with visitors because of the distrust and hatred they've encountered from many outsiders, earned and unearned.

Protocols dictate the etiquette or correct behavior in any given situation in a culture. They are not morally right or wrong, but rather what is practiced in a particular culture. For instance, in the Philippines, you never pass between two people who are talking unless you bow your head and make a prayer-like gesture with your hands. I learned this in missions class and practiced it soon after the class, in the Philippines. It is polite. In Afghan villages, you eat with your hands, but it is impolite to get rice above your wrists. I learned this from my Afghani student. In the United States, you do not eat with your hands except for certain "finger foods." Very impolite. I learned that from my grandmother. Neither is right or wrong, but both are simple etiquette in a given culture.

In Kosovo, a young woman serves chai (tea) in order of the importance of the person. It is served from the oldest man to the youngest boy and then from the oldest woman to the youngest girl. I learned this from a Muslim family that welcomed me into their home in Kosovo. Protocol again. In the United States, two people talking will keep a two-foot space between them. Getting closer than that, even among friends, is just not polite. We learn these cultural codes of behavior by observing social relationships as we grow up. Rarely is anything said; you just observe it and then copy it. If you ask why something is a certain way, someone will tell you it is polite.

One of the first prison protocols I learned is that you never ask a man's crime. Charlie told people about his, knowing that they sometimes needed to understand. But he was the exception, something I discovered when I asked about another inmate.

"I don't know what he did to come here," Charlie said.

"You just told me he has been your friend for years."

"We don't bother with what the crime was. They are here and that is enough."

Dishonest men will lie, and honest men often want to forget what they have done. It is hard to have to explain their crime to each new person who comes along. Often they have had the media go over and over their crimes on the five o'clock news and in their local newspaper enough for a lifetime.

Charlie helped me understand another reason to withhold information about one's crime. "That's the one thing a man can keep to himself if he chooses," he said. "Thoughts are private and no one can drag them out of a person; they are things over which the inmate has control." The crimes are all the same, in one sense, because the crime is what got the inmate inside. Similar to the Lord telling us sin is sin.

One thing all prisoners have in common is *doing time,* waiting out the years until they are given probation, are paroled, are pardoned, or die. We all have experienced long seasons of waiting, although most of us haven't thought much about it. We wait anxiously for weddings, birthdays, graduations, anniversaries, and other events. As children, we did time as we waited for Christmas. Thanksgiving night, I would race to our old "stereo" record player to put on holiday music. My parents would not allow us to play Christmas music before Thanksgiving night. From that time on, it was almost unbearable, waiting for Christmas morning and opening presents. We even had to wait until after everyone woke up. Someone had to make coffee for the adults, and then we were "released" to open our gifts. My grandfather loved to witness this. Every Christmas morning, he would go from one bedroom to another waking us earlier than usual, enjoying our excitement. *The joy of release!*

Obviously, getting done with a prison sentence far exceeds any Christmas anticipation for those inside. People who are getting out soon will say, "Three weeks and a wake up," meaning three weeks and the morning when you wake up. Who can imagine what that must be like for long-timers? A person thinks about it more or less constantly, especially as his release date nears. For some, their sentence is complete when they leave. Others get out on parole or probation, which means they're still under supervision by the Department of Corrections. Others only leave the prison by dying.

Try to imagine waiting for Christmas seemingly forever, with no end in sight for years and years. Living under the roof of "Corrections," but no matter how good your behavior, no visit from Santa Claus. That's what doing time feels like for Charlie and other long-timers. They will all leave prison someday, but it may not be until they die.

Maine has not had parole since 1976, so there is little hope of release for someone with a life sentence. Even states that have parole don't always administer it well. One woman in New York, going for a parole hearing, said it this way: "Before that fourth hearing," she reflected, "it felt like it doesn't matter what I say. It doesn't matter who I am or what I've done. It's never going to change; the crime will never change. The hard part about it was that I'd changed."(This woman finally did receive a parole date. Her name is Diana Ortiz, and her story is told in a *New York Times* article by Trymaine Lee, "Convicted of Murder as Teenager and Paroled at 41.")

Many years in prison will eat away at a person's soul unless they learn how to do time well. Some work at getting an education; some work at avoiding problems by buying a TV and watching it all day. Some "sleep their time" so they do not agonize about their situation. Charlie did a course that he loved on the Bible. He also spent time building relationships with others in the pod and in the yard. Once we met, he spent a lot of time writing to me or visiting. And of course he worked for a living so he would have some money to get things he needed or bless others with gifts.

Often, when outside people are blinded by a desire to just get a man who commits a crime inside under lock and key, they are in effect compounding the problems for society. Doing the time is the punishment, but some staff take it on themselves to punish more while a man is inside. Evidence-based practices show that recidivism (the tendency to relapse into criminal behavior) will go down only when and if there is support, respect, and program changes, as well as a good parole system. Many staff members told me that Charlie had "done his time." That means they felt he was indeed corrected and good to leave. And more than that, he should have been allowed out by home confinement, or clemency. Maine had very few options for long-timers, having struck parole off the books back in the 1970s.

Doing time is done well when someone faces what he has done to get into prison, makes amends, and regains self-respect and the respect of others. "The best course I ever took in prison was Victim Impact," Charlie told me early on.

"Why?" I asked.

"Well, we had to sit at a table with victims and families of violent crimes. A psychologist or psychiatrist led it, along with a volunteer who just loved on us. One person who was a victim of violent crime was busy blaming me for her pain. I obviously did not do anything to her, but I learned through the anger I felt toward her. I also heard her pain and understood some of her pain and anger. It was the hardest course I ever took too. It actually made me face what I did. Really face my guilt."

"That is awesome," I said.

"It was awful painful. There is still not a day goes by that I don't think about what I did, but I have truly done everything I can think of to make amends."

Perhaps one of my first revelations concerning prison as a culture had to do with language. Charlie used many terms I did not understand. As with any subculture in America, prisons have their own shortcut words and descriptions that save a lot of unneeded talk in getting to the point of a conversation. *Chow hall* is a term with the same meaning as it has in the armed services. The men at a prison go to a chow hall to eat meals. Sometimes they *eat in,* which means their food is brought to their pod or cell because the walk to chow hall is too much, usually because of a medical condition. Two opposite terms are *on the street* and *inside.* Charlie would often say, "When I was on the street," meaning when he was not in prison. He would say, "On the inside," meaning this was something that happened inside the prison.

My house was a term I was polite about for a long time. I would desperately reason with myself that it sounded like he meant his cell. I thought he was ashamed to call a cell a cell. Charlie used the expression, "I went back to my house." Calling a cell a house was unimaginable to me. I concluded it was indeed his house, just as I had been writing from my house. The chief difference was he never called his cell his home, while my house is very much my home.

I learned protocol about writing to a person in prison. People inside do not share with other people what comes in letters. Sometimes I would write Tiny a small detail of my week, and then, rather than tell the whole story again to Charlie, I would ask Charlie if he knew the particular thing I had written. "No," was his consistent answer. Charlie only knew what

I had said to him. Tiny did not share it. And of course vice versa. Like their thoughts, their letters were private.

In the postwar culture of Iraq, Bosnia, and Kosovo everyone spoke of *before the war* and *after the war,* much as we now speak of *before 9/11* and *after 9/11.* Prison also has its own timeline. Time begins with *when I did my crime;* time ends with *getting out.* And everyone does get out, eventually. Measuring a span of time, someone will speak of a year after "I did my crime" or "two years before I got out." The sentence itself defines a place in history. This realization astounded me. I began to get a little bit of a picture of how prison defines a life forever.

Charlie's childhood culture on the outside virtually disappeared when he was incarcerated. For example, most of us have a history of our life in photos. We have a few from our childhood and more from our teen years, high school graduation, weddings, and family. Going to prison for life, an inmate sometimes loses this record because he is not allowed to enter prison with personal things. A portion of his life is gone. A prisoner's family will either stick by him or totally cut him off. Wanting to be rid of memories of the pain caused by the person inside, family will often toss out personal effects along with pictures left behind. A man in for a long sentence often loses all contact with his history, including, understandably, his family. The shame of the crime is something the family wants to go away.

"My wife stayed around a long time, but finally I knew she had another life, and I drove her away," Charlie told me one day.

"I'm sending you some pictures of my family," he told me. Charlie had a few photos of his life before prison, but most of his family history remained only in his memory. I framed the few he sent. There is one picture of his mother, older at the time, sitting in an armchair at home. His father is quite a bit younger than Charlie in the photo I have of him. It was taken on a beach somewhere. And a favorite is his grown son with a huge fish he caught, obviously after Charlie was incarcerated. I have photos of almost every special event in my life. Charlie had few photos of his life events.

The prison restricts how many pictures inmates can have in their cells. How do prisoners tell their children and grandchildren their history without photos? It is reminiscent of immigrants leaving Europe for the United States years ago. Space was limited on ships, so pictures and other precious family items were often left behind. For Charlie, this loss of identity because of his crime was another hole in his life.

While in prison, a person also loses all right to privacy. One day Charlie told me, "I have a metal box," indicating a size around two feet by eighteen inches by eighteen inches, "for storing my things. And that is not private. They come in and go through it every time they think someone is hiding a shank (a handmade knife) or drugs."

Not long after we began writing letters, Charlie said, "They will be reading every word, so just know that."

His freedom to write and read letters meant only for him was gone; his freedom to have a private conversation with me on the phone or at a visit was gone. Our conversations were "subject to monitoring," as the automated voice reminded me each time Charlie called. (Though we did not do phone calls for many years, eventually our relationship progressed to the point that Charlie would call me. That change would come with some conflict and heartache, in fact—but that is a story for later.) At the end of the voice message, they told me I could just hang up if I did not want this call, and I could press zero if I wanted to talk—in that order. The details almost always show an extreme expectation that the public will not want to interact with inmates, even though prison administration is aware that interaction while in prison helps lower recidivism rates when people leave prison. And the vast majority of inmates do leave prison before they die.

In an emergency, I could not call Charlie unless the social worker decided I had an emergency. This too is part of prison culture, a stripping away of one's personal life, taking away important outside participation. When my last surviving uncle died, I wanted Charlie to know, so I called. They had to get all the information, what relation the uncle was to me, where he lived, what funeral home he was going to, and all that before they would have Charlie come to the phone and call me back—all while I just wanted him to know so he could pray for me.

When someone on the outside says, "Felons should be punished more," I realize that person does not appreciate the extent of the punishment the people inside already have. Recent studies confirm that isolating someone from society typically leads to more social and emotional problems—just another part of prison culture we do not comprehend. And it *adds* to recidivism. (You can read one such study at http://www.usatoday.com/news/nation/2006-06-07-solitary-confinement-study_x.htm.)

Charlie accepted the fact that this loss of privacy was for security reasons. He said, "It's just part of life in prison." But understanding that did not make it any easier.

On one visit, Charlie said to me, "A woman guard was watching me showering once. I told her to quit gawking. Told her to get out of there." It is beyond me why a prison would have women guards for men in private moments like that. It's a needless affront to common decency.

Charlie worked at being honest with inmates and staff alike about issues that came up between them. Often he said to me, "Some guys come complaining to me, but I tell them go tell that guard or that person. I have always told the truth, to guards and other inmates alike, and they respect me for it."

The prison rules brought other needless irritations. One example was the address I put on my letters to Charlie. He had a unit number of 400 when I first started writing him. Eventually someone told him he could not get my mail unless the unit number was listed as 500.

"You gotta put Unit 500 on the letters now," he said.

"Why?" I asked over the phone. The word foolish came to mind. He was in the same place as before.

"They said so, and that's just the way it is." From experience, he had learned that to argue over such irrationality takes a lot of valuable energy. Perhaps it would be easier if they took time to explain some things, but I imagine a man inside for decades would not care. It is just another seemingly capricious rule. One fellow inside recently wrote, "You know how it is in here. Rules change every five minutes." That's how it feels.

I did start using Unit 500 and continued to do so. Because of the power they had to withhold my letters to Charlie, I did what they wanted. I often wondered as I mailed a letter, *Will it get to him this time?*

One way for administration to encourage positive doing time is to have routines and rules that are consistent. How frustrating it is each year to find out the IRS has made new rules and I learn only at tax time that I could have done something different to help myself. To have 24/7 life rules that are about every conceivable thing changed all the time, changes even made by a guard in a bad mood, wears away at one's sanity.

After some time, I learned that Charlie could receive books and CDs as gifts. I sent him one for his birthday or Christmas—a CD from a distributor—and it was there at the desk for me to take back when I left a visit one day. It was marked contraband. Someone in the prison had used a CD to fight another inmate, and instead of just going for the offender, they made this a new rule: no more CDs for prisoners. For Charlie it was extra hard, since he knew it had been a great effort for me to send him a gift only to have it given back.

When letters come into prison, they rip stamps off because drugs can be hidden under them. For the same reason, there was sometimes a rule that return address labels could not be used. But for the whole time we wrote letters, the rule changed back and forth. It was allowed and then was not allowed and then was allowed again.

"I don't care, as long as they stay away from me. I will do it until they change it again. They have a new rule, I point out it was this way yesterday, and they say 'do it.' I do it," Charlie said one frustrating day. I have heard him also comment, "Some guys just choose to do their time that way, arguing. I choose to stay out of it. I still mention that it was not that way yesterday, but I don't argue." His attitude was more or less, "I will let you know that I know this does not make sense. I will not ignore that it does not make sense, and I will let you know I am still alive enough to know it is important to me that you know I know."

My struggles with the prison rules and the harshness of his circumstances did not help matters for Charlie. It was just another way I unwittingly brought the outside in.

When I told stories about my life, Charlie would sometimes grow quiet and thoughtful. His life had narrowed to a very small piece of real estate, while my life had expanded from New England to the whole world. My stories would remind Charlie that he had literally lost much of his past. Memories too painful for words were provoked by the mere mention of something I did. For example, if I wrote about one of my children, it often brought up thoughts and longings in Charlie to see his children. Charlie had two children—sons—from his first marriage. They were brought to visits when he was first in, but not often. The relationships had been wounded by his alcohol use, by two divorces, and of course by his crime. He soon resigned himself to never seeing the boys again. One son continued to write every so often, but it had been over a decade now since Charlie had seen him.

Charlie Speaks

I've seen many changes in the prison system during my years inside, and sadly, many of those changes haven't been for the better.

When I first entered the Maine prison system, I was sent to the old prison at Thomaston. It was small compared to prisons today, and some of the facilities were in bad shape. But we had an administration that seemed intent on giving inmates a sense of personal dignity. Things were better for me and others back then. A place of contentment, if you could ever say that about prison life. Most guards were good to us if we were good to them. We were allowed to earn money and were able to work on our own projects, not just projects for the state. Items made by inmates were sold at the Prison Store.

I decided to learn wood carving. Creating ducks and other wildlife helped me escape into a different world. As I carved, my spirit soared beyond those prison walls. I could escape without leaving the prison. I could go to the backwoods, the lakes, the ponds, and just feel the joy of nature. I could go off to God's country.

So for the next fifteen years I carved my way through the lakes and ponds and deep woods of Maine, places where I had been so many times as a young man. It was truly wonderful, a very peaceful time. I even taught a few other inmates along the way. I had no idea that God was working on me through what I was doing. But He was there all the time.

With our earnings, we were allowed to buy food for once-a-month cookouts. These picnics gave us a chance to break bread with other men and just enjoy the day. Now, this may be hard to believe, but we had some great times. Friends would gather together, eat to their hearts' content, and talk about good times past. Talking about the past is part of doing time.

For those cookouts we could buy almost any kind of food we wanted. Hot dogs, hamburgers, salads, chips, cold soda, and ice cream sundaes loaded with all kinds of good stuff were on the list. Some men bought fish and chicken. It was a different world; that's for sure. These outdoor times lasted for many years. During the winter, we could order out once a month for fried chicken, pizza, and different types of fast food. All of the food was bought by the inmates, so none of the cost was on the state. We also had different bands that would come in with all kinds of music. It was a grand time for all, the guards as well as the inmates.

All that changed with the coming of the new prison. The population went from four hundred to nine hundred-odd inmates overnight. The system was not yet ready for that many inmates in one place; the older and younger all mixed together. The increase of drugs and gangs in prisons across America made officials more and more worried about security.

We lost so much coming to the new prison at Warren. At the old prison we could buy our own clothes. Today we have to wear uniforms that cost a huge sum, something taxpayers do not need. But the administration wanted to make a change. We lost all the cookouts; they would not let us have them anymore because there are so many inmates, and inmates are feared more than we were at the old prison. Not that they were not on the lookout at the old place, because they were. But there were not so many to watch.

The incidence of drug use is a lot more than at the old place. Handling the younger inmates is difficult, more so than it was years ago. The drugs that they have are also different. These drugs are brought in many different ways, and when one way is found out, they find another way within a few days. It is a never-ending cycle. That is part of life behind the walls, and many need the drugs to do the time, to get through each day. Inmates now hold a lot more feelings inside because of the harm that has come with the changes. There is less talk and more action, meaning fights and using more drugs. How do all the drugs get in? I cannot say because I have no proof. I really don't want to know.

Making money has changed. We can no longer work for ourselves. We have to work for the state or not work at all. We work for an hourly wage, and what we are paid depends on what we are doing or what they feel we should get paid. How is this preparing us for outside where you can work hard and earn a lot? We never were in control, but it felt like we could do something.

Things would be better if the wood shop was more open so that the inmates had more say so in it. That will not happen again because the system does not trust us. Respect is gone.

We no longer have a prison canteen where we can buy different kinds of food, only personal care items like soap, deodorant, stamps, and shoes. But no food whatsoever. All our extra food we buy out of machines at a very high price. What a shame we cannot work together. Doing time would be so much better.

Many of us older inmates would like to be back at Thomaston. Yes, it was not as clean as this place, and the rooms were not as big. But there was so much more to keep the inmates busy.

We live by rigid codes that we did not have at the old prison. A red code means fire. We are locked in for that. A blue code means a medical emergency. Someone is down or hurting. We get locked in for that. An orange code means someone escaped, and we get locked down for it. Never had to do a lockdown at the old place.

Even Kairos has been affected. During the beginning at the old prison, there was plenty of food brought in by the outside people. Women would bake cookies, brownies, and cakes. But all the food that was brought in was stopped at the new place.

I must say that God has really played a big part in all of this. He has been there each day. He opened my eyes to His love and greatness. He has always been there for me, even though there were times when I felt

He was not. I was often angry and blocked God from coming through to me. This is an angry place. Sadly, a lot of hate in here is caused by the inmates' pasts and by the way things are run.

Charlie persisted in having me ask questions in letters, and he responded openly to everything that crossed my mind. Understanding the culture helped me to understand the man. Ultimately, as we wrote about important areas of our lives, the cultural differences grew smaller. But first we wanted to share some things about his crime as well as his childhood. It was time to get to know Charlie on an even deeper level.

Chapter 8
CHARLIE'S CRIME

As I continued to share with Charlie my past troubles with men, with each letter and visit I probed a little deeper to learn about Charlie's life before prison. "Growing up in the woods of Maine was a great life for a kid," he said. "I loved to walk the woods, exploring and fishing and doing all the stuff boys love to do. I felt so alive and free out there, a lot like the deer and loons that lived nearby. I am part Mi'kmaq, or what I would call Indian."

The Maine woods became Charlie's refuge from his turbulent life at home. His violent father and whining mother made life unbearable at times. He and his sister, Rachel, grew closer as they tried to survive in this messed-up family. If they got into trouble for something, Charlie took all of the punishment, meaning he got beaten for both of them. "Rachel was older than me, but pretty fragile both physically and emotionally. I wanted to protect her."

In response to my tentative questions, Charlie continued to answer all he could remember about the events leading up to his crime. I felt a combination of anger and nausea at the story of wreckage and horror that emerged. More so as I realized he also felt nausea and anger at what he had done. But I had to know.

"When I was ten, some kids in high school came after me. My sister and I were going out for Halloween, and my father told us not to go to a certain part of town. It wasn't right but I went anyway. Made my sister promise me she wouldn't tell. I was just a kid. I met up with some older guys; these guys had knives. There were three of them, one girl and two guys. They made me take off all my clothes below my waist. Said they were going to cut me up," he shared with a strange combination of bravado and shame in his voice.

Charlie obviously still felt violated and humiliated, all these years later, so I didn't probe for more details. He kept talking. "The girl told them awful things they should do to me. I got away, but I made a decision. I vowed to never ever let anyone overpower me again."

He went on to tell me several family incidents that had left him scarred emotionally. Sometimes I wondered if he even knew that parents usually protect their kids. He said he began sensing there were family secrets that no one ever spoke about. Shame seemed built into the family culture, even about things that did not matter. His parents were always more concerned about how the family looked to neighbors than about how they really were doing. He was often severely beaten for infractions that might reflect on his parents' reputation. Although I was not beaten, I'd had the same feeling about my family and their reputation. Maybe it was just their generation.

Charlie said his breaking point as a young adult happened when he came to his folks' house to see his sister, and they were hesitant to say where she was. He had been out of their home for some years at that point. As the conversation went further, he knew they had not planned to tell him that she was being treated for mental illness.

"You were not going to tell me Rachel's in a state hospital? What kind of family is this anyway?" he yelled.

He had already turned to drinking away his troubles, and that turned into more troubles. "What started as me defending myself or my sister became a plan to not let anyone control my life. Fight after fight evolved into my life of anger and control." Soon his first marriage ended, leaving two sons with a heritage of pain and violence. After marrying again came a series of incidents that spun his life totally out of control.

A bombshell was placed on the family: Rachel committed suicide. Charlie had long ago confronted his parents about how their lack of love had affected Rachel. Now she was gone. Along with grieving the loss of his delicate sister, Charlie still had to deal with his demanding mother. He said she wouldn't take any responsibility for what had happened. "She blamed a woman who worked at the bank for the suicide."

He dulled his searing pain and anger with more alcohol. "A year before that I got in a fight at the mill where I worked. When I left the hospital they put me on a lower type of Valium. The doc gave me the Valium to help me calm down. One day I was in the kitchen working on an old-fashioned stove, putting in new rods. I turned around, and there was a figure standing there. It was a huge threat to me. I had a big hammer. I got mad and threw it at the figure. When the hammer hit the wall, I came back to reality. It was my father. I had just missed him. They just gave the Valium to you back then with no supervision. If you had more pain, you took more. I had no idea how dangerous it was. Don't think *they* did back then either."

Later, in the span of one week, he separately ran into both of the men who had sexually abused him as a child. He said they had no idea who he was, but years of hurt erupted from within Charlie's gut. He threatened each of them, one in a public place.

Meanwhile, day after day, his mother harped at Charlie about the suicide. She insisted that the woman at the bank had cheated Rachel by not depositing all the money she brought into the bank that day. "She said Rachel's husband was furious about the funds disappearing. That's why Rachel committed suicide," Charlie said. He did not think that made sense, but he kept listening.

"Understandably she was grieving the loss of her daughter," said Charlie, "but most of all, she wanted it to be someone else's fault. Actually it was Rachel who did it." Charlie was still sorting it all out as we talked.

"You could at least defend her when she is not around," his mother bellowed. "Go do the right thing by your sister!" His mother repeated that several times.

"So I decided to go talk to the woman from the bank. I didn't know what good it would do. It certainly wouldn't bring Rachel back, but I thought it might stop my mother from whining."

Charlie bolstered himself with a handful of Valium and set out for the woman's house. "Before I left I had been popping pills all night. I had pain in my head, maybe imaginary. But I made up my mind to go see the woman, go talk to her."

Reason with the woman, he thought as he traveled to her house. He realized later he should have stopped right there. It was none of his business. But back then, he couldn't see it. *I will face her and talk about the missing money.* Anger grew. *I will shake her up a little so she will admit it,* he thought. *That way she will understand she caused Rachel's suicide, and maybe there will be peace.* He was not thinking clearly.

At first, the Valium calmed him, but by the time he reached the woman's house, he was hallucinating. "A doctor told me later I was lucky to be alive because of all the Valium I had taken. Hallucinations started about the time I got there. The room was huge. Then her hand grew as big as a house. I was tripping but had no idea the drugs were doing that to me. At first I was angry, but all of a sudden the anger turned to fear of the woman," he continued. "The room grew still and my fear went deeper. I grabbed a knife and stabbed at her hand, but hit her arm. That is the last thing I remember."

The fury of those next few blank minutes he would regret for the rest of his life. "Later the psychologist told me I grabbed a knife and stabbed her numerous times, did terrible things to her. He said that the hallucinations probably made me think I was protecting myself."

But as fast as the hallucinations came on, his mind cleared of the drugs as reality set in. With a trembling heart, he looked, and with sudden understanding, knew he had killed her.

"I can't tell you the horror I felt, the awful pain. I instantly wished that I was the one who had died. I kept thinking, *I didn't mean to kill her. I don't even remember it. I just wanted to scare her.*"

Knowing how fast the law would respond to a big crime in a small rural town, he said he thought about running away and hiding in the woods. But he decided he would face what he had done even though he was scared. And the futility of escape, and forever having to look over his shoulder, was not like Charlie Page.

He would face his demons. Numb with bottomless shame and sadness, he left for home. Whatever would happen was out of Charlie's hands now. He prepared for the inevitable arrest. "When they brought me in for questioning I played games with them for fear of what was going to happen to me. But before the day ended, I admitted to the crime."

He had taken a life with his own hands, and facing her death was the most difficult thing he had ever done or ever would do. Everything in life as he had known it ended that day. The justice system now took over. Being from a poor family, Charlie had no way to hire a lawyer, so a public defender was appointed. "I was told that if I went before a judge, without a jury trial, I would avoid a life sentence. I could explain to the judge what happened."

Doing as advised, Charlie talked to the judge. Later he was surprised to receive the very sentence he was not supposed to get: life. But he did not flinch, not even when he found out that Maine had recently become a "no parole" state. He would literally spend his life in prison. He did not care. In his mind, he was getting what he deserved. Devastated does not begin to describe the feelings that were traumatizing him. He could not get the thoughts out of his mind and the picture of her lying there. Then there was prison.

Instead of working with the programs for anger management that Charlie was taking, geared to change and correct him, some staff taunted and teased him about his crime. "How many times did you stab her, Charlie?" was one goad several morbid staff members used to try to get his ire up.

For at least five years, Charlie was out of control most of the time. But the futility of this eventually led to a time of deeper hopelessness. There were good and evil practices that went on inside the prison; Charlie had no choice but to submit to them all. He learned to sit when they said sit and stand when they said stand. When he changed prisons, from Thomaston to Warren, things got worse.

He wrote everyone he could in his little town to ask forgiveness for what he had done. He had to measure each person, knowing that some were too close to the wave of destruction he had created. He worried that writing them would bring them even more pain. He did his best, going forward by asking forgiveness from most of those he had hurt and letting them know just how sorry he was.

"I was not following Jesus at the time, but I knew enough about God to ask for forgiveness. I also started praying for this woman's family and friends, along with my family. They were all devastated, destroyed really. God did not feel real, but I knew He was there."

His family just stopped coming to visit. Charlie's dad had died before the crime, but his mother was alive when I met Charlie. However, she had not visited for very long into his sentence. Charlie came to realize he would have to make it alone or not make it.

Twenty years after his crime, Charlie still had no relief. Knowing that only he was to blame for the crime, he nursed a hurt so deep inside that he could not even speak of it to friends. In this place of total brokenness, God was faithfully drawing Charlie to Himself. It was at this point of genuine and desperate devastation that Charlie attended a Kairos weekend and became the man Bill had mentioned who was so big and wept before the Lord.

"After a Kairos reunion meeting in Warren, I got back to my house, and a letter was there. It was from a woman very affected by my crime. She wanted closure. I had told her as best I could what happened and asked her forgiveness. In this letter she told me she had forgiven me a long time ago. She had forgiven me for everything. I just didn't know what to say or how to receive it. I don't even know how to tell you. When I got her letter, I guess I once again felt like a human being."

Thanks to God's amazing grace, Charlie made it. It was a long journey up from the pits of hell, but he pressed through the despair to find new life among the supposedly worst of the worst inside the prison walls. The man I had met and started visiting was indeed a new man, radiant proof that God changes men. But being made new is not easy. And daily regret hung in his heart.

Chapter 9
OTHER PEOPLE'S KIDS

My awareness of justice system problems started way before I met Charlie. When I was home for short leave from Kosovo, a friend invited me to go to the Long Creek Youth Center, a detention center for kids up to eighteen years old, for chapel one Saturday. I said yes, and off we went. Going became a routine each time I was home.

I mentored a couple of young men at Long Creek, connecting with them each time I went to chapel. Each inmate had received a jail sentence for a certain period of time, but good behavior earned them points toward more responsibility inside and early release. Once they reached level four, they could go home. Often we talked about what they planned to do once they achieved level four. I knew they needed a plan. Many kids inside had trouble reading, a skill they needed to survive outside. I taught reading. It was a way to inspire them to set goals of going to school and getting a job. A Learning Disabilities teacher working at Long Creek once told me, "Your student was recommending you to everyone in there. What are you doing?"

I also became involved in a major project in my neighborhood. After selling my condo, I moved to a poor neighborhood and began renovating a house built in the late 1800s. That left me no time for volunteering at the youth center, but God brought troubled kids right to my door. My lifelong passion has been helping troubled children. Kids were all around the place I was renovating, and they were all looking to meet the new lady on the street—to size me up, I suppose. These kids were kids with parents in prison, kids who had been in jail, kids on probation, and kids in trouble. They told me all that when they found out I was writing and visiting someone in prison. Charlie had also fallen into helping some of the younger inmates since his own children were outside. We both knew love was the key to helping them change, but I could never find enough love inside myself for all the kids I encountered before I met the Lord. Now I discovered this wonderful thing: He multiplies love, and His wellspring never dries up. Hurting kids get better and heal faster when touched with the love of the Lord. *His* love is what they've been missing.

One day Charlie said to me, "You know that neighborhood where you are living?"

"Yeah?"

"Well, I checked around and found out it is the biggest drug center in southern Maine."

One young man Charlie met in prison told him about buying drugs at a house on my block. Mike wrote a letter telling how drug abuse had shattered his life and led to crime that landed him in prison. His mother read the letter at the opening of The Shed. Mike's letter to the kids who lived around me was passionate. He urged them not to make the mistakes he had made to earn prison. When the town official we had invited got up to speak, he said a little and gave up. He was so moved by the inmate's letter that he could not go on.

I hadn't known about the drug problem in my neighborhood until Charlie told me, but it made sense of the number of police cars that were always circling around! A Sanford policeman confirmed Charlie's information. Later, a youth pastor at River of Life told me about a conference on drug trafficking that he had attended. He said, "Kay, the drug people are decentralizing from the big cities. They bring drugs into a small place not far away from the city with a small airport and a relatively small police force." His description fit what I knew of Sanford. We are only eighty miles from Boston.

Society embraces an image that people in prison are all incorrigible, that they and their families are part of a new group of untouchables. As I lived out my life here, speaking of my visits to see Charlie and calls from him, many friends and neighbors opened up about their loved ones inside the walls. Our community policeman was someone I could call as a first line of help. I wanted to make sure we were following the probation rules too, since many of the kids were talking openly to me about court-ordered curfews and other rules. These kids all hung out together and talked about probation, but usually not in front of adults. Some kids were allowed out by their probation officers after curfew if they were at The Shed.

Our dream was that it would be a safe place for the kids, and they were coming from all over town. Furthermore, we wanted to see kids break away from old patterns of criminal activity and find out that they could live without acting out antisocial behaviors.

The Shed also became involved in the Angel Tree program at Christmas. Founded by Chuck Colson's Prison Fellowship, Angel Tree offers a way for a person outside to buy and give presents—on behalf of an inmate—to that inmate's children. The program gives the names of contacts to various churches so participants can find out the specific needs of each child.

One year I brought gifts for two sisters who had a Sanford address. Having the mother's name and phone number, I called and set a time to deliver the gifts. The names sounded familiar, but the house was quite far away from my neighborhood. When I drove over there, I was very surprised to hear, "Hi, Miss Kay. Mom, it's Miss Kay from The Shed." In this family both parents had been incarcerated, but at the time the mother was home. God was bringing kids from all over town to us at The Shed.

Our community continued to grow. I became friends with several women from Sanford who were seeing a husband or boyfriend on the same day or days I visited Charlie. Two were from my neighborhood. It was good to meet others close by who had a deep understanding of what it was like to have someone in prison.

As part of my outreach to the kids, I decided to go and meet with a person from the district attorney's office and the juvenile probation officer. I thought building a relationship with those directly involved with these kids would increase our effectiveness. The day before that meeting, I found a DVD at the library about learning-disabled children. Out of my old love for kids with reading problems, I brought it home to watch. This was where I first heard this startling revelation: the DVD said the decision of how many cells to build in virtually any state is partially based on the fourth-grade reading level of children in the state. Let me restate that.

When a state is considering building a new prison or jail, virtually all can better predict how many cells they will need by looking at the fourth-grade reading level of kids in that state. Again, if the kids in a state are not doing well in reading, it predicts more jails or prisons will be needed. As a reading teacher, I was horrified.

The next day I met with the DA official. "Okay," I said. "I saw this story on a DVD yesterday." I related the story of the prison/school connection.

"Yes, that is why I took my kids out of public schools," he told me.

I could hardly wait to tell Charlie. At visits he was always talking about the system, meaning the prison system, and I was also always talking about the system, meaning the school system. This was huge in my mind because I vaguely remembered that way back in the training I had first received in intensive phonics, the teacher had said that jails were full of people who could not read. Statements like this about jail somehow stuck out in my mind because it reflected a real desperate need for good reading practices. Suddenly the Lord was connecting the pieces from the past with what was going on with Charlie in the prison system.

Since I was not going to other countries often anymore, one of my fervent prayers was that kids from this neighborhood would rise up and go on missions trips. Some thought that I was expecting too much, but I knew God could do it. One kid came to The Shed as a very angry young man. His father was in prison, although he refused to talk about it. But gradually he changed and normalized. In working with traumatized children, I have learned that they become normalized by hanging out with children with positive goals and input. This boy eventually moved, and after getting involved in his own neighborhood church, he stopped coming to The Shed.

One day he came up to me in the grocery store and said, "Guess what I am doing this summer?"

"What?"

"Going on a mission trip," he smiled.

One highlight of the work was to discover that my alma mater, Wheelock College in Boston, had announced a meeting concerning children in trouble with the law. It was part of their recently added juvenile justice program. They had invited a judge to come and speak on the topic. I wondered if others I knew were involved. I was the first one to arrive that evening! Wheelock has always been a leader in innovations with children. They had put up with me, their student, as I joined the civil rights movement in the 1960s. At the time, they were consulting with people in DC about a new idea called Headstart, a program that would help preschoolers from low-income homes get a head start in school. They had even catered to my desires to work with children in at-risk situations, placing me in a kindergarten in a tough Roxbury neighborhood for student observation. Starting with my love for children of any shape or size and adding a passion for kids with a problem, I learned to figure out a way to help. There were no pat answers for kids, and I learned not always to accept the norm but to develop a program for children who did not fit a particular mold. In our "seminars" back then we did not have methods prescribed, but we looked at the child and multiple methods to find solutions for kids. Later I was surprised that other teachers were taught "methods" courses. We were expected to think! I had also received a background in child development that had no equal. I knew for sure that children were not born criminals. Now I realized that poor teaching of reading was somehow connected to people being arrested.

Intrigued, I took the whole matter to God. *Okay, Lord, this reading/prison connection is huge. And You have me talking to this big guy who can read and write but is in prison. How will all these pieces tie together, Father? I can surely see Your hand.*

Little did I know how God was going to tie together some of these things in an uncomfortable way for me—and not in America, but in Kosovo.

Chapter 10
GOD'S PLOT IN KOSOVO

N o, I am not in love," I said when Carrie Sue asked.
"But you are so happy whenever you see him," she replied. "Your
face lights up when you talk about Charlie."

Fear of a deeper relationship frightened me; romantic connections
for me automatically meant being hurt. Been there, done that, and have
many T-shirts. Furthermore, this man was in prison, not exactly the usual
setting I had thought about for romance. It just could not be. Carrie Sue
and I were going to Kosovo in the summer of 2004, and I just did not
have the time to sort this out.

"Have you contacted the translator?" Carrie Sue asked me.

"Yes, and he will pick us up at the airport. Don't forget to plan on
money to give to him when we leave," I reminded her.

"I cannot wait. I have wanted to go on a trip for so long. Besides, I
feel like I know the translator and the family we are staying with. Also,
can you give me a list of things for us to bring for the kids? We can ask
people in church to bring things for us to pack." She had done this very
thing for me many times, and now she was organizing things for herself
to bring.

Charlie and I had talked about the trip at an earlier visit. "I'm planning another mission trip, Charlie. Carrie Sue and I hope to go to Kosovo.
Not sure when."

"That's good. I will be praying for you when you leave. It's still dangerous there, I guess."

"Yes, Serbs and Albanians are still fighting on the bridge that divides
their territory. The people I stay with live right by the famous bridge that
separates the two sides. Carrie Sue wants to meet my Kosovar family. We
want to pray on the bridge. Carrie Sue wants to meet Evan and his family,
the Roma family we adopted, too. She has done so much to help them."

Charlie's prayers meant a great deal to me as we prepared to go. When people say they will be praying for me as I go, I am humbled. I am only the point of the arrow. Prayer people and financial providers are all part of the team. Some of the prayer giants from the prison were joining me as I went this time. Praise God.

Bags packed and treasures for the children ready to distribute, we finally boarded a plane for Mitrovica. Carrie Sue and I could at last talk for hours about our lives and our dreams as well as pray through the city together.

We had met years ago in a church in Waterboro. Both of us had a strong love for the worship time there. After she moved into the same area where I lived, she and I took our first prayer walk—in three feet of snow. We worked our way toward each other and met in the middle. She was trained as a teacher, and she had also become involved with the reading program I used to bring so many kids the ability to read.

"I like our translator," she told me after we arrived in Kosovo. He had driven us to the house on Hairizi Street in downtown Mitrovica, a city still fighting using guns and fear.

Not wanting any incidents with the Mujahedin, we stayed at our host home most nights during our time there. Huddled in the safety of our room we could talk and pray for hours. We sat on the two daybeds at one end of the room; there was a kitchen of sorts at the other end. Using candles for light after 6 p.m. when the power went out lent a mysterious air to some of our ponderings.

"So, I think you sound like someone in love," she started in again.

"I don't know. I have thought I was in love so many times with other men. You know that. And the biggest thing is that this cannot be because he is in prison."

"I know," she assured me. "And Kay, he is in an awkward position to say anything. Maybe you should just discuss the level of friendship. You know you are good friends with him. He is helping you sort out a lot of stuff in your life. And it sounds like he enjoys you coming."

In the midst of occasional interruptions from our host family, we discussed and prayed over every aspect of my personal dilemma. We also prayed for our planned prayer walk on the bridge over the Ibar River.

"Today we are going to Evan's house," I told our translator. He was used to the routine, taking the money to the Roma family as well as a bunch of needed food that they would not otherwise have.

"Our translator knows the foods we need to buy to do Kosovar cooking," I explained to Carrie Sue. She was busy sorting out some of the kids' items to bring Evan's children. She had waited so long to meet this family and had prayed for hours for them. Before we left she had collected many items for everyone. At last we would bring them over to the family.

I can still see Carrie Sue's face change from curiosity to deep kindness that first time we went to Evan's house. Evan had been cheated out of the brick home he was building on his land by an unscrupulous lawyer. Having ten kids to raise with no job or money was a challenge. He had found two-by-fours to build the room where they stayed while he had been working on the brick structure. After covering the two-by-four walls with cardboard, he topped it with a huge blue tarp he probably got from the UNHCR (the United Nations High Commissioner of Refugees).

The room often smelled of some sort of heating oil, perhaps kerosene. It was midwinter when I had met him a few years ago and terribly cold. This summer, the three of us were invited in. The heat was unbearable, attracting flies to the food we'd brought. At home we take screens for granted, but this family had never even imagined a screen. Reflecting on the poverty of this family, we knew that for Evan, living with his wife and ten children in one overcrowded room was hard. I sometimes found myself becoming immune to the sadness as I had spent so much time with people in war-torn countries. In the dark it was difficult to even see the children hiding in the shadows. But I *could* see the tragedy again, as if for the first time. Love was mirrored on my friend's face. Looking at Carrie Sue reminded me to care again.

On the way back through the colorful market place that day, we were treated to a visual feast. Our translator had gone on his way home. The oranges were almost red, bananas plentiful, greens were all piled high under the awnings. Many Albanian mothers were out shopping and bargaining loudly for their daily food needs as they wrangled with their children to behave.

"Look," Carrie Sue said as we came out the other side of the market. "Is that a Mujahedin?" Her camera was already coming out from her purse.

Pulling out of a side street was a long cart with a man riding on it like a cowboy in an old movie. Mujahedin were easily spotted by their dress and the full beards on their faces and signature cap on their heads. Their pant legs were always a bit too short, so that white socks were visible beneath the hem of their slacks. By now we were just across the street from the market.

Carrie Sue carefully took a picture of the Mujahedin, who promptly became a very angry Mujahedin! His eyebrows suddenly were closer to each other, arching in the middle at the moment his mouth twisted into a scowl. A loud volley of Arabic words escaped his mouth as he turned his attention to us, and we did not need our translator to tell us his fierce message.

"Let's *go*," I said emphatically. We walked quickly back through the protection of the marketplace and as fast as possible to the room we were renting from our hostess.

After such a close encounter with this man, we entered a desperate appeal to God about our planned prayer walk. I had no way of knowing how close the network of possible terrorists or at least anti-American people might be who had come to take advantage of the conflict on the Ibar River. But these men who had just recently started to show up on the sidewalks I had walked now for five years appeared menacing. Now the madness of the city had become real for Carrie Sue as well.

After NATO entered the conflict in 1999, the whole of Kosovo was divided between Albanians and Serbs. North of the Ibar were Serbian towns and south were Albanian. The city of Mitrovica itself was rich in lead that provided battery manufacturers with their main ingredient, causing many to want to run the mines. The city was bisected by the river. Therefore, the connecting bridge had been a place of constant mortar and gunfire.

Some of the little children I worked with in the city were Albanian but lived in a northern enclave surrounded by Serbs. They were trucked daily to and from schools on the south side by military convoys—cattle cars. We ministered to war-traumatized children who were often retraumatized as they got on the cattle cars provided by NATO troops. They came to join those who lived on the south side to go to school and spend time before and after school at one of the three Sonshine Clubs that we ran there. The Serbs on the north side were also traumatized by the war. Unfortunately, we were not equipped to deal with those on the north of the river. River of Life International was a tiny organization.

In prayer, Carrie Sue and I had thought that we were to cross the Ibar River, praying, and then continue to the north side. From there we could pray silently as we walked. We had a strong desire to at least pray for the Serbs and put our feet on the land as we had already prayed for the Albanians. But real danger could lay ahead for us in our strategy as we crossed the famous bridge that next Monday.

"Kay, how did you feel about the Mujahedin today? It was pretty scary," Carrie Sue commented.

"Well, mostly I feel like we need to pray into it a lot more," I said, grossly understating it to break the tension for my friend and me.

She was shaken, but willing to do what we felt the Lord was leading. Armed conflict was still going on, often at the face-offs and fights on the bridge. And so many people hated Americans. In particular, the Serbs disliked us because the United States had led in the NATO invasion. I had had several slurs uttered toward me by Serbian people.

In prudent preparation, we e-mailed people at our church and people in Kairos requesting prayer for us at a certain time on the next Monday. In that letter I mentioned that I would like someone to tell Charlie Page to ask his friends to join us in prayer. The message went out on a Saturday, and we were walking on Monday morning. I had figured the time difference and told people exactly when we were heading for the bridge, Maine time. God bless the invention of e-mail. The prison chaplain, Matt, made a special trip to the prison on Sunday to give Charlie the message which someone from Kairos had forwarded to him.

On the big day, Charlie, along with his buddies and many other prayer partners, supported our undertaking with their prayers. What a treasured memory to know this ally of mine was praying for us and stirring others to join him in asking the Lord for our safety! I was touched deeply by the care and understanding these men had for me out on the field. Charlie inspired them.

"Let's get moving," I said as we prepared to leave the house. "We either get in trouble or don't, according to what the Lord allows."

I had ridden in the cattle-car school convoys with the children after visiting with parents on the north side several times. The invisible border, punctuated with razor wire on the south side of the bridge, had always brought me relief when I came back south. As we would leave the Albanian conclave near the Workers Monument on the north side, the children would whisper, "Miss Kay, don't talk until we get there." I loved to be singing silly songs to the kids. Or just talking. They peeked out holes in the canvas sides of the cattle car to monitor our trip back to the Sonshine Club Center. Finally getting to the razor wire on the south side, we would know we were home free. These kids were literally smuggled from their home in the conclave on the north side to their school on the south side and back every day. Some as young as nine years old had to come before school started when the convoy left but had to wait at the Sonshine Club so they would be supervised until school started.

A total change of atmosphere engulfed us when we approached the bridge that Monday morning. At the other end we would go right around the Dolce Vita Café where the Serb leaders met. There was a sense of danger. As we walked past all the cars that were parked by the bridge, we could see the razor wire placed there to bring a measure of protection to each side at the entry to the bridge.

As Carrie Sue and I looked over the side of the bridge, the typical red-roofed European homes looked peaceful enough. Even the imposing buildings on the far side did not seem to be a threat, although we knew the Dolce Vita Café at the entrance to the north side was a meeting place for war strategists.

In the distance, armed men sauntered out along the bridge with the air of bullies as cars and military vehicles crossed slowly over on business. No one would make any sudden moves in this no man's land. My head had already had its fill of the honking horns and the inevitable smell of exhaust that follows military trucks, a mainstay on the road across the Ibar.

War countries remain dangerous long after the war is over for various reasons. Law breaks down in a war zone, and men begin to occupy themselves with becoming amateur police. Many of the self-styled law enforcers gathered closer as we neared the north side. Menacing looks and people noticeably shunning us gave the message as we kept walking: "We don't like you and we don't want you here. Go away." Our feet were marching but our hearts were yielded to the Lord, who was indeed listening to our meager prayers.

The wannabe cops thrust their guns forward to let us know they were a force to be reckoned with when they saw we were women alone. Some people, less daring, registered their disdain by walking literally and deliberately to the other side of the street. Remarks were made in their native language, but by the tone of their voices we knew we were in a potentially explosive situation.

People from both the Albanian and Serb sides were there, each angry because we sought to go from one side to the other. The NATO forces wanted them to mingle—Serbs and Albanians. As we prayed for peace, Carrie Sue and I sensed our mighty God was right there, holding us in His hands. Moments like these always make me know that God enlists prayer partners back home for a good reason. We could not have done this alone.

"Boy, they were not nice, happy-looking campers," Carrie Sue offered.

"No, this is the scariest walk I have taken ever here," I said as we neared the infamous Dolce Vita Café. Gearing up for the most difficult part, we kept moving forward. We were now in the unfamiliar territory of the north side. I knew the Albanian conclave from doing teacher training there, and I once been in a Serb conclave in the south, but I had not walked much on the Serb streets on that side. This day would have been terrifying if I did not know the Lord heard me from the ends of the earth.

If possible, the spiritual atmosphere grew even more hostile as we continued on the northern land to walk around the block Serb side. Most people in European countries recognized us as Americans. This day was no different. Several older women, heads covered in old-fashioned scarves, commented with disdain on their faces to us. Some spat on the road near them, indicating no love.

As we walked past the tall buildings on the left around the buildings housing the café directly across from the bridge, the height alone seemed to cower us. But there were children, a welcome sight. Prayers for each of them and their families came to mind and were uttered silently with every step we took. Kiosks selling bits of peanuts, candy, and trinkets the children loved were an obstacle to get around, and we stepped carefully over the constant clutter of a city under siege. Even our nostrils were assaulted by the stench of garbage untended along the sidewalk.

From the bridge into the territory on the north side of the city seemed a very long hike. We walked the whole way around the first block and back to the bridge. If we could have measured our steps it probably would not have proved long, but our hearts were well worn when we finished. We knew the walk had not been in vain. In not backing down, we were somehow showing the love of God to all the onlookers. That was the victory in our prayer journey that day. Later, at the house, we were relieved to just talk about it all, going over every threatening detail of the prayer walk. Both of us were glad we had done it, but it took a toll on us.

When I got back to the States, I set up a visit with Charlie.

"Hi there. How was the walk?" He obviously had taken the prayer covering for us seriously. And he was as glad to see me as I was him. "I loved the postcards. Imagine that. All the way from across the ocean to *this place.*" Charlie often called the prison "this place," implying a forlorn outpost of despicable repute. "Sit, and tell me all that happened."

We spent the two visits that day going over all the details and then praying in the afternoon. He caught a bit of my heartache for the people we had left behind as we prayed.

Sharing the details of the trip, the dangers and the joy, felt like I was sharing with a favorite brother. His delight at being part of the story was to be a new experience for me. He really did care. And he had loved getting his first "e-mail" hand-delivered by Chaplain Matt.

As I talked it all over with Charlie, I realized that our prayer walk across the bridge had been the biggest spiritual battle of our journey. And through it all, by prayer, Charlie and his friends had been part of the battle.

What would God do with all this connectedness I felt to Charlie?

Chapter 11

LOVE, CHARLIE

Y ou need to talk to Charlie about your friendship."
I did not like Carrie Sue's prodding, but I knew the Lord was using what she was saying to confront my fears.

The friendship issue now echoed through my thoughts daily. Was the Lord pressing me to bring it up with Charlie? How could I explain it? What would I say so he would not think I wanted to marry him? I prayed. Fervently. Desperately. Women of my generation just did not start a conversation of this nature about relationships. Every time I'd tried to bring it up or write it, something inside me screamed no, no, no!

Eventually I found the courage to write to Charlie about the change in our relationship as I saw it. I said, "Charlie, I feel like our friendship is deeper than I expected. I would like to define it if we can. Could we talk about it?"

It had been easier to face an AK-47 in Montenegro than to mail that letter. But mail it I did. Sink or swim. I felt a sense of relief at having faced the fear of what he would think and my fear of rejection. If he wrongly assumed I was in love with him, so be it.

Next came the agony of waiting for a reply. Day after day, I paced back and forth to the mail slot. When a letter with his familiar handwriting appeared, I snatched it and tried to quickly squelch the racing of my mind. *Just sit down and read it,* I told myself out loud.

I hurriedly poured myself a cup of coffee, put my feet up on the coffee table, and sat back to open the letter. I would now know what he was thinking about our relationship. What I would know was not clear, but I would know something. I could not admit—even to myself—the true nature of my feelings because that would mean I was vulnerable to a man. But Charlie wasn't like other men I'd known. I had made myself open up to him.

I read, holding my breath.

He said I was never to come visit him again, and please write. He said I was an outsider and outsiders never understand, and please write. He said he did not know why he had ever let me come in to visit him, and please write. By the end of the letter my whole body shuddered. I had to set down the coffee.

Total rejection. He was candid as he could be, but it was my deepest dread realized. He had totally rejected me.

Confusion. Shock. What? My mind fought to recognize the words on the paper; they were totally unanticipated. I could not laugh or cry because I could not even comprehend. Several readings later, I began to sort out what Charlie had written.

I should never have written that letter. Again and again I read the lines, hoping that somehow the words would change. The realization that I had been rejected—and humiliated—by still another man crept into my consciousness. Ugly, angry feelings mostly aimed at myself. Now what?

Lord, I must have really heard You wrong this time. You knew what I was planning, and You are big enough to stop me. Why didn't You!

Ugly and angry now toward God. I was so angry at God, and I let Him know. I figured He was big enough. When I finished my rant, He sent peace to my heart. I picked up the letter again.

Okay, I see there are three times he asked me to write. It still feels like rejection, but I will write something back. I just have no clue what to write now, I thought. My precarious position was not to my liking at all, but finally I knew I had to follow through on my commitment to write to this man. This friend.

Asking God for courage, I began working through what I needed to say to Charlie. First, I asked forgiveness for having upset him. I also said I would honor his request. No more visits. I closed with a few details about my day just to try to keep a friendly tone. Then I sealed it and sent it off to the prison. It was not long, but it said what I needed to say. It was all I *could* say. Writing more words seemed pointless when my heart ached so much.

October 2004 seemed the longest month of my whole life ever, or at least since I had met Charlie. Visiting him had become a big part of my time, and seeing him in person had suddenly ended. Everything in me wanted to do a fast slide into depression, but I found consolation in an upcoming family reunion. My children lived all over the eastern United States and Canada, so I was pleasantly distracted with the coming gathering of our tribe.

Two more letters from Charlie came that month, and in both he seemed to be distancing himself from me. However, each one asked me to keep writing. I answered them both—briefly and without enthusiasm. Stringing it out like this seemed foolish, but I would continue to write as long as he wanted.

After my family left, I thought more about what he had written. Disturbed by what I perceived to be anger in his correspondence, I called Dan, a man Charlie saw as his best friend on the outside. After a brief conversation with Dan's wife, Linda, I was invited to come see them. Once together in their warm comfortable home, I blurted out all that had happened.

"I've done something that really hurt Charlie, but I don't know what it is. I feel like I've invaded some private culture in the prison and made his life unbearable."

I felt big tears rolling down my cheeks. Their first response to me was overwhelmingly kind and gracious. I never felt the slightest bit foolish baring my heart to this astonishing couple.

Then, quite unexpectedly, Dan laughed.

"Dan, why is this funny?" I asked, confused more than ever.

"Kay, he is just fighting with his feelings. Prison life makes a man feel closed up. It's hard for him to face what he is feeling."

He has feelings? Are they good? Are they bad? What does "he has feelings" mean? Why is he fighting his feelings?

I did not dare to ask Dan all my questions. It was getting late, and I had to drive home. But underneath all my denial, it dawned on me that I *wanted* Charlie to be in love with me. But I was not willing to be in love with him. In battling my own feelings, I had stuffed the thought of loving Charlie, and maybe that was exactly what Charlie was doing. Oh well. I had to just wait out what the Lord was doing—if He was indeed doing something.

Another white envelope arrived a few days later, with the now familiar stamp on the outside saying, "This correspondence is from an inmate at the Maine State Prison." It had come through my mail slot and was lying on the floor. I decided to leave it there. Over the next several hours, I walked by it several times, each time the letter daring me more loudly to open it. I had read his three letters this month about me not coming to visit. And I had written back. What more did Charlie want? Wasn't the shortness of my letters getting the message to him?

Oh Lord, I do not want to be in this position. I am crumbling.

I ignored it. I'd had all the rejection I could handle. I was not going to let another man pierce my heart. Talk about protection! I would *never* allow this. No one would get in there again. Absolutely no one. Not even Charlie Page. Finally, having gathered up enough reasons why I was not going to care anymore, my inquisitiveness got the better of me.

What does he want now? I thought as I opened the letter. *How will he push me away this time?*

The words this time were even more stunning. Would I forgive him for his harsh words in the letters? Would I come and visit again? He said the Lord was showing him that I was just a loving person who wanted to talk about our relationship and was not a threat.

The next letter in November was even more stunning.

Kay, when you decided to help me to get out of prison you cannot even think how much fear came over me. Now you want to talk about our relationship. That was the straw that broke the camel's back.

I really let go and drew back inside myself. I started to backslide and really got scared that I might get out. Please understand that I really want to get out but it was very real when the fear came over me. What would people think of me after what I have done to go to prison?

I know it is all in my head, and the Holy Spirit is working

on me to come to understand that. I cannot do this on my own, and I need to let Jesus lead the way. Fear is a sin, and I will not let it take hold of me any longer. I need to talk to you. What do you say? Let's fight this with Jesus's help, okay?

…I want you to set up a visit for you and me as soon as you can. Saturday morning. Is that okay with you? I really miss seeing you.

And he signed it "Love, Charlie."

I was not rejected! I did not know what I was, but I was not rejected. Of course, we had lots more discovery ahead of us.

Chapter 12
LOVING RELATIONSHIP

L ike diving into the ocean in the summer, I did not know how warm
or cold it would be, but I dearly wanted to swim. Here I was diving
into relationship with Charlie again, sink or swim. It did dawn on
me that when in a very early letter he had asked if I could help him on
the outside if he got clemency, he might have already been thinking we
might be an item. I had been clueless. All I knew was that the church
would help him.

I set up a visit as quickly as I could and prayed for God to help us
talk this out. Nothing would be traditional for us. It could not be. So I
guessed we would be making things up as we went along. Right now I
had no idea how to say what I wanted to say to Charlie.

"Oh, hello, Charlie. I just realized I am in love with you." "Charlie,
are you madly in love with me?" It went on and on. Of course, none of
the above was appropriate. If I really loved him, I would let him decide
how to handle this. Maybe.

What does defining a friendship mean anyway? I had finally admitted to myself that I wanted him to be in love with me. And that last letter
had been amazing. Creeping in logically at this point was the thought
that maybe I was in love with him, as Carrie Sue and Nanda had said. I
knew I loved being with him, and guarding my heart was getting
exhausting at this juncture.

Once through the intake process at the prison, Charlie greeted me
with a warm smile but no hug. Every time he opened his mouth, I
expected him to take the initiative and bring up the subject of defining
our relationship. The theater in my head said the man starts this conversation, not the woman. And besides, I could not even form a question in
my mind. What would I ask? How could I phrase it? For a good half-
hour we talked about the weather, the noise level in prison, my ride up,

and his job, and all of it did not matter one bit right then.

When I made up my mind that this discussion would happen, I took the cold plunge. Charlie told me later in the coming year that when he had written something in a letter about us meeting at Kairos, he had also made up his mind to make something happen for us. Two stubborn people. Anyway, I finally broke in and asked, "Charlie, when are we going to talk about our relationship?"

He burst into one of his reverberating belly laughs. Then, seeing the startled look on my face, he said, "Now." And further, "I never in my life met a woman who would talk like that."

"Like what?"

"Ask honestly."

I giggled, but more from nerves. Well, it sounded as if he savored my daring.

"I don't care for games, and if there is an elephant on the table, I will mention it," I told him.

"Me too," he said.

"Okay, what is God showing you?" I wanted to know.

He replied slowly, seeming to count each one of his words. "I think that He is going to do something very deep between us." No levity now, just peaceful reflection on what was transpiring.

"Something deep" was too vague, not the answer I had expected, but I decided I would leave it alone and allow him the next move. It sounded like he *had* acknowledged a deeper friendship, and I realized I did not want to go any further at this moment. I just wanted to enjoy our whatever it was.

Razor wire was still visible outside the window of the visit room; cameras were still in the ceiling watching our every move; and we were still sitting behind the walls. But we felt freer in our relationship than ever before. How this would work was a big puzzle, but we were enjoying each other right there at the visiting table. Guards were watching and not seeing, people visiting and not paying attention, and the clock ticking its time. This was not passionate infatuation, but we had a sure sense that God was God, and He would show us His way.

"God has this all in His mind. He will lead us," Charlie reassured me.

I just nodded my head in agreement.

We dropped the subject at that point, knowing we each needed time to ponder it—by ourselves and away from the other. We simply enjoyed every single minute of our visits for the rest of the day. Though we had four hours together, it seemed like minutes before the words rang out, "Visits over." We hugged good-bye as we had done so many times in the past. My brother who was my friend had become my brother whom I loved.

We both prayed intensely that week, and I drove back the following weekend, eager to hear what the Lord was speaking to him. Somewhere in our conversation at that visit Charlie used the word *marriage* and opened another door. As soon as it was said, I knew the Lord had spoken.

"What do you need most now in life?" I asked.

"Well, I asked you before to be my hands and feet on the outside. You have done that always. But I need companionship mostly."

"Me too," I agreed. This was first on our lists. Definitely not the passion of youth, our desire was for the assurance of enjoying each other's company into old age. Emotional and spiritual connection to another for life was a desire we both voiced.

Lord, You planned love this way. Slow, sure, and gentle. Your ways are not our ways. Thank You.

As Charlie leaned over to hug me good-bye, he gently kissed me.

Immediately I was seventeen all over again, but with my feet firmly planted in loving the Lord. The tender acknowledgment of our new relationship marked an answer to our need for sweet companionship. In the bleak month of November, my heart soared to warm, golden heights.

New Year's Day 2005 came, and I visited. A phrase had slipped into Charlie's vocabulary a few more times since the day we had spoken of our new relationship: "when we get married." I had heard it several times before and ignored it. I wasn't going to let it pass another time.

"No one has asked me to marry him," I said, looking him right in the eye.

"Kay, will you marry me!" he practically yelled with a twinkle in his eye and a trace of being fed up in his voice. Okay. It was not quite the romanticized proposal I had pictured, but nothing about our relationship was traditional, and I truly did not care. We both laughed.

"Yes," I replied. We were engaged.

Chapter 13:
PREPARING THE WAY

O n the drive home from the prison, my mind raced with the implications of what we'd just done. How would my pastor see this?
Would the people in my church accept it? Would our children be
able to understand this, and then the grandchildren? How could we support ourselves financially, either way? Would the ministry to children at
The Shed have to close because the director was married to a man in
prison? If Charlie were to receive clemency and be released, would he
be allowed to talk to the children on my street? Would the neighbors be
in an uproar over a felon living next door? A tremendous number of
unknowns came to mind. But above all, I knew in my heart that I sincerely loved Charlie, and we would move mountains to go forward with
the marriage. It had been such a long struggle for both of us to get to
this point, and at our age I suspected he had gone over all the possible
doubts as I had. More than once I mentioned to the Lord, *You do know of
course that he is in prison?*

Charlie had been so kind and gentle and so committed to me. Off
and on during renovations on The Shed and the house he would advise
me what kind of workmen to get for what project. To call the house a
fixer-upper when I bought it would be a gross understatement, but I had
learned to trust Charlie on what to do in different stages of the process.
Now we were both going into another fixer-upper—could we renovate
our life patterns and make a successful marriage?

Charlie was beginning to show signs of being very trustworthy with
my heart as I shared more and more of my hurt from other men. One time,
as we were talking about me hiring a man to replace the windows, Charlie
wanted to tell me something about fixing the ones that existed. I looked at
his face, and my eyes were watering with the anxiety of wanting to please
him and still wanting to get the good windows. I wavered between getting

new ones and pleasing him instead. I overrode him and decided to get the new ones, and I had the distinct feeling he was putting my feelings above what he thought was possible and less expensive for me.

"You know what will work best, Dear," he said. "I am with you on this." His response was so different from what I was used to. He supported me rather than coming in macho with all the reasons I should not do this. I could hardly wait to become one with this tender man.

Clemency was our great hope. After we decided to marry, Charlie asked for an application for clemency. I had no idea if he would get it because I knew nothing of the law or the possibilities. But I was certainly willing to help, to try. The marriage was going to happen either way, and romantic that I am, I wanted him home for the wedding.

Two years earlier, Charlie had asked me if I would help him work toward clemency, the only legal channel for his release. I had no idea what this would involve, but I said I was willing to do what I could. Now it took on new importance for me.

Clemency means legal mercy. Mercy is not getting what you deserve as punishment for a crime; it also means getting what you do not deserve. Never hiding his guilt, Charlie had pursued change in his life for many years. He had now served twenty-odd years of a life sentence. He would formally ask for mercy from the governor. It all seemed so simple; Charlie was a changed man. Many of the prison staff testified to that. By now I knew some of the guards, and they would tell me about Charlie's changed life when I was alone in the lobby with them. Surely, the governor would grant mercy and release him.

In my online research, I came across a doctoral thesis that included a history of clemency. The first recorded mention, according to the author, was when the Roman governor Pontius Pilate asked the crowds to choose either Jesus or Barabbas to be released from prison. Only one of them would be granted this gift, and the people would choose. Pilate made his decision, not based on mercy, but on politics. The author of this thesis remarked that clemency had been this way ever since—a political decision. At last, I had an understanding of clemency that satisfied me. But it was not good.

Finally sensing that this was no simple matter of the governor being a merciful man but rather a political problem, I faced it. I asked a lawyer friend what he thought the odds were for Charlie to get out. "Oh, zero," he replied. My response was, "I am praying for God to release him and believing for a miracle."

He laughed and said, "You would be." I began to recognize that it would indeed take a miracle. Charlie also warned me that clemency would not end his legal problems.

"I will also be on probation for the rest of my life, if I come home," he explained. "I will be a suspect for any crime that takes place nearby. They would be able to raid our house at any time."

"Well, if they want to, I am too old to care. I have nothing illegal going on at home," I laughed.

To start the process, Charlie gave me the name of a woman who used to work in the prison wood shop and was now an assistant commissioner. She had to get written permission to discuss him with me. With that arranged, I visited her to ask for help in understanding how clemency worked. She said, "At best clemency is a long shot. If there is anyone who should be out, it is Charlie. I have never seen such a dramatic change in a man, ever. I am glad someone is helping him and caring about him." She did not know we were engaged at the time.

I did not know it then, but she was the first of many officials connected with the Department of Corrections who would share this thought with me.

Charlie continued to work filing the clemency papers and requesting the documents required by law. "Can you write to as many Kairos people as you know to get a letter for me?" he asked.

"Of course," I replied, and wrote myself a note to do that soon. I gathered names of other people he knew, asking them each to write a letter of recommendation.

The reality was that I would continue traveling that long road to the prison for the foreseeable future. I thought I might sell my house and move up closer if the driving became too much. But then I wondered how I would leave all the people I love and who were so supportive of

Charlie and me at the church. But I was getting ahead of myself.

"What if you don't get clemency, Charlie?" I asked one day at visits.

"I don't know. Only way is to try, and leave it in God's hands." I knew he was right.

"Can you do life with me if I can't get out?" he asked.

"I have no idea, Charlie. I really don't know a lot. I guess if God gives an okay to all this, He will give me the strength to walk out our marriage. I love you so much that I want to say yes to that. But we have to face the obvious concerns. Like I don't know if I can go on without being beside you at night; tender companionship is what we both want. And neither one of us is a prize in the area of marriage." He smiled a conspiratorial smile.

"My biggest concern is you letting the outside in. Will I get upset with it all the time once we are married? I just don't know," he shared in a private moment.

"Well, I keep reminding God that you are in prison. I don't know what else to do. It seems like He is telling us to do this."

"Yeah, I know."

I talked to Charlie about more concerns and said I wanted to submit our plans to my pastor.

"Ray has been my spiritual leader for years now. I know he hears warnings from the Lord for me. I cannot marry if Ray gets a red flag."

Charlie did not mind that I would be deferring to my pastor. If the Lord wanted this wedding to happen, Ray would give his blessing. Putting everything in the Lord's hands through Ray was wisdom, and I was determined not to have another fiasco marriage. For either of us. Charlie actually jumped at the chance to trust God in it all. After all, we were now on a spiritual journey together as well as an emotional and physical one.

In reality we would go on seeing each other even if Ray did not agree. But we both wanted to be one under God. We knew there was benefit in this even if we never could be together at home. There would be special blessings even if we did the whole life sentence.

Telling our children was priority, but asking our pastor for his blessing was the first step. We did not want to concern the kids if the marriage was not going to take place. I put in a call to Ray.

On the day of our appointment, I did all the usual pleading and agonizing with the Lord before an important event. Approaching my pastor with our plans was unnerving, but I knew he would listen and give wise advice. If Charlie and I were totally missing God, Ray would know from the Lord, and we would call off our marriage. Ray was our protection. He had served in that role for me for years already. For example, at one point in my career as a missionary, I was sure that I was to go back to Iraq. In my meeting with Ray, he got a very strong NO to my going. A week later, war broke out again in Baghdad.

"Don't ever bring me anyone you want to marry unless he is strong. Stronger than you!" Years before Ray had given me his warning. He knew I needed someone tough since I was tough.

I walked into our meeting not really knowing if the Lord would give me dear Charlie in more than just friendship. If God was going to stop us, I wanted to deal with it fast.

"Ray, I have something to share that will bring more trouble to you and the church," I began.

"That is normal for you," he joked. Ray asked the Lord to be with us for whatever I had to say.

"Well, you know the guy I have been writing at the prison and have visited for a while now?"

"Uh-huh."

"He and I think the Lord is telling us to get married. I have never met anyone like him, but we agreed to let go of it if you get a red flag."

"Oh. That's different from what I expected. But I suspected you were in love. Marriage is forever," he said. "Can you do that?"

"Of course, I don't know. No one knows how it will go, but we did everything we could to come up with a reason why we should *not* get married. We were our own devil's advocate. Charlie talked about me 'letting the outside in' and how difficult that's been for him at times. He knows I have been reminding the Lord that he's in prison. We also talk a lot about our rocky marriages and what we learned from them. We know marriage is a lifetime commitment, and difficult as it will be for us, the Lord still seems to be pushing us along this path. We hope he will be released some day. We are going to apply for clemency."

I noticed Ray praying quietly on and off during our meeting. He had pastored me with an ear to the Lord for many years.

"Charlie and I have been writing since 2002, and we enjoy each other's company. He is patient with my foibles. I try to manipulate him, but he doesn't budge," I said with an ironic laugh. I gave Ray a brief history of what had happened to make us think the Lord was leading us.

"Have you talked to him about what happens if you do not get clemency and what you will do then?" I could hear genuine concern in his voice, reflected in the somber look on his face.

"Yes, for a lot of hours in the last few months. We have decided to put it all in the Lord's hands. Also what to do about telling all our kids. We figured we would talk to you first, so if it was off, we would not need to burden them. The bottom line is we have to trust God. Isn't that what all of us have to do when we make a commitment to marry?"

"Kay," Ray said with urgency in his voice, "will *you* be able to do it if Charlie has to spend the rest of his life in prison?"

"I honestly don't know. We talked about it, and God is able. I am praying that I am willing." I had not been this serious in my whole walk with the Lord. Silent cries to God for wisdom were strewn all along our path to marriage.

Ray nodded. Then I caught a glimpse of fatherly concern on his face in spite of our very slight age difference. He was going to get out the big question.

"I want to know one last thing, Kay. Is he strong?"

I smiled.

"I think so. Come meet him and judge for yourself."

Ray promised he would, and he quickly sent in his application to visit.

When Ray's application was approved, I set up the meeting. Ray would follow me to the prison in his car. Our plan was to meet with Ray for the morning visit, and then I would talk to him at lunch. He would leave and I would go back to see Charlie and tell him what Ray had to say.

We left early, and I occasionally lost visual contact in the misty predawn darkness. When I called his cell phone, Ray assured me that he was close behind.

"Your driving is all over the place, Kay. Speed up, slow down, speed up." He laughed. "Just ease up. Relax."

"Yeah," I said, "I know. I am nervous and afraid I will lose you." I was also nervous about the decision being made for me that day. I didn't want anything to keep Ray from making it to this momentous meeting.

I finally calmed down when we got to the visit room. After we signed in and waited for the visit to start, I introduced these two very special men in my life, and they were off and running. Soon Ray was describing his past life on the streets of New York City and how he got the scar on his neck. Charlie was telling his war stories from his tiny country town. Jokes and laughter rang out inside the cold cement walls of MSP, and I was on the sidelines as they sized each other up. It was a grand visit!

The two men obviously enjoyed their time together. It was definitely man talk, and I was basically an onlooker. As we left to our respective lunch places, Charlie joked with a twinkle in his eyes, "I will meet you guys at the restaurant."

Once we settled for lunch, Ray said, "I see no reason why you should not marry. I like him, he's fun. He's honest. And he *won't* let you bowl him over. As far as I am concerned it is between you and the Lord."

Near the end of the conversation, I asked the next burning question on my mind. "Now, what happens when your director of missions announces she is marrying someone in prison? We know this is not the usual turn of events."

"I suspect the Lord will start tweaking your ministry and you will be more geared to people in prisons or people affected by prisons," he replied.

Wow, was that all? That would be fun! I had expected this to be a time-consuming discussion for Ray and me because this was a life-changing decision. Truthfully, I had wondered if I would be able to work in missions after I married Charlie. Instead, Ray encouraged me to follow what the Lord was saying. My heart sang. I was sure my face glowed with delight.

That afternoon, I brought the good news back to my future husband. "Charlie, Ray thinks you are good for me, and we are fine to get married if the Lord continues to lead us."

Lord, I am grateful, so grateful. I will follow Your lead. Could You confirm this new ministry direction?

Within a week a young man who lived near me approached, saying, "Miss Kay, will you come to court with me? I got arrested last night."

"Of course," I said.

The Lord was confirming my future with prison work. It had been almost three years since I began writing to Charlie. Now it seemed my involvement with the justice system was about to get much broader. I thanked God that I could be a support to this kid.

Desperately we wanted to share our good news, but we knew it would be a curious marriage and perhaps not such good news to our kids. But they had to be told.

"When do you want to get married?" Charlie asked.

"I think quite a ways off. What are you thinking?"

"Well, September 3 would be nice," came his instant reply.

"Oh, your birthday. So you can remember. I get it, Mr. Page. You are already afraid you will forget the date, huh?"

"Yup," he replied with a boyish grin.

"We better do it then. And you better not forget!" I ended that discussion.

"What do I say to the kids?" I asked, looking for his input.

"It will come to you," Charlie joked. He had no more an idea than I did.

My five children and their spouses are a free-thinking group of people, and I really wanted them to be happy about Charlie in my life. But would they be?

Chapter 14
REVEALING OUR MARRIAGE PLANS

It's funny how time and experience change your perspective. On my first visit, the Maine State Prison seemed like such a scary place. Now sitting in its packed visit room, everyone looked quite normal, including those incarcerated. However, I knew it would not be easy for family and friends to see my engagement to Charlie as "normal." To some it might seem crazy at best, dangerous at worst.

I concluded that they would have to do one of two things with this news—think outside the box or distance themselves from me. Of course, some would be concerned because Charlie had committed a violent crime. I knew this because I had also held in my heart every type of stereotype about men in prison, especially those who had committed violent crimes. Some would no doubt advise against marrying a man with a life sentence in prison. Who had ever heard of a happy, fulfilling prison marriage?

Sadly, Charlie had not seen either of his two sons for at least ten years, so my children were the focus of spreading the news. I dreaded making these calls but hoped I could convey to them the joy and fulfillment that Charlie and I were feeling. Just to accept that I would marry again would be hard for my kids. I couldn't gauge how they would react to the news that I would marry someone in prison.

The first call was to my daughter Camelia in Canada. She listened silently as I explained how this relationship had developed and how we felt God was leading us.

"Oh, great," she said. "Now I will be writing a book called *My Mother Married a Murderer.*" She was trying to joke with me, but my heart ached for her and her family. This would be more difficult for them than I realized. Being connected to a person in prison was an unknown for my family. I had to acknowledge their responses and just keep loving them.

I told Camelia I was leaving it up to her what and how much she wanted her children and husband to know. I promised I would visit them in the spring and talk more then.

Charlie, of course, understood her reaction and appreciated her honesty. He was the first to say that forgiving murder is very difficult.

When I arrived at Camelia's place a few months later, my bed was in the living room, surrounded by toys and books and a lovely view of the lake across the street. The next morning, my six-year-old grandson Obadiah came in to talk to me, looking quite serious.

"Grandma, I heard you are going to marry a murderer."

Oh, my goodness, could I deal with Obadiah's forthrightness?

"That's right. I am."

"I don't think God would like that."

"I think He does. In fact, I think He told us to get married," I countered.

"No, He doesn't like murderers."

"He loves everyone," I said. "In His Word He put lots of stories about people who murdered other people. He says to kill is really wrong. But God still used those people in His greater plan."

"Who?" Obadiah demanded, with a tiny doubt in his voice.

"Oh, Moses. And Paul. He killed Christians. And David," I replied.

"No, not David. David did not murder anyone," he argued.

I answered, "He had someone murdered. You can read it in the Bible. Have you ever done anything wrong?" He owned that he had. "And when you did that, were you sorry?"

"Yes."

"Then what did God do?"

"He forgave me…oooh. I get it!"

That was the end of that particular discussion. Obadiah had a pure understanding of what God said in the Bible about forgiveness, and I was amazed once again at God's care for me and for my grandchild. Not all adults would be this accommodating.

Obadiah and his sister Lindy went off to work out this new information through play. They hung dolls with ropes and poked each other with toy swords all week. And then, as children do, they accepted it. One step at a time.

Telling your parents you want to marry is a difficult task; telling my children I would marry was proving even more daunting. It took me a month to call every one of my children. Each call, I had to pray and then get up courage to deal with the unknown. I left it in their hands as to what to do with the news. And during our visits, Charlie and I prayed for them even more. Our hearts were broken that I could not include his kids in this process, difficult though that would have been. We included them in our desperate praying.

I gave Charlie's address to those who asked to correspond with him. In case they were fearful, I suggested they use their church address as a return address. This protects the person writing because people in prison have harassed others when they were let out, and yet a legitimate return address must be on an envelope or the prison will not deliver the letter. I knew Charlie would do no harm, but the address could conceivably get into the wrong hands inside. I explained what could and could not be in a letter. No glitter. No tape. No glue. Basically just ink or pencil on paper.

"Of course you know that everything you write to him can be read. I just want you to know what you are getting into if you decide to write," I told them. "Security is a priority."

Their questions and comments were thought provoking and challenging. They each chose a different path concerning our marriage.

My son Aaron responded politely but with no enthusiasm at all. He is an out-of-the-box thinker, so I was not expecting this. When I asked if he wanted to meet Charlie, he simply said no. At first I thought his unwillingness was due to Charlie being in prison, but the next time I saw him, he wanted me to go see the famous prison in his town. It turned out he was upset about me marrying after a divorce. Gage, my oldest son, was happy for me but distant. I think he just did not know what to make of it. Or figured I was crazy.

One of my children, Tracey, filled out papers to visit right away and came to meet Charlie as soon as she could get to my house. She is quiet, but her coming spoke volumes to us. Later she would meet the love of her life. The test for him when she first knew him was what would he do after he found out about Charlie and me. He passed and became instrumental in enriching our lives.

Charlie just took life as it happened because he did not have many choices, and yet he was fully aware of the perceptions held by the general public about people in prison. He harbored the same prejudices before he became a prisoner. Introducing Tracey to my intended was possibly the most intimidating step of all. Charlie delighted in her as he did each one he subsequently met. He said, "I have always wanted daughters." He was grateful to everyone who came to meet him.

My son Todd was open, but due to his precarious marriage, he was not able to talk much out of respect for his wife. In the end he too came to meet Charlie.

Later, Josh and Camelia wanted to visit Charlie for the first time, along with their children. If we could work out the problems, they wanted to come. The two children carry EpiPens with them for severe allergies, so we had to work with the prison security people.

"The grandchildren need the medicine with them," I told them. "They cannot visit unless somehow the meds can come into the room with them." The staff at the prison worked out that Camelia could bring the medication to the desk in the lobby. The rover, the guard who escorts us, would bring the packs with the prescription down to the visit room and the meds would stay with the officer overseeing our visit, so if needed we could access the life saving EpiPens quickly.

Just days before Josh and Camelia finally left for the United States, we had a big discussion over the phone about what my grandchildren should call Charlie.

"How about Grandpa Charlie," I offered. I knew Charlie would not care one way or the other.

"No, I want them to know their blood grandfather as Grandpa."

That was fine with me. Whatever she felt was right, was right. For the time being, we labored over another way for Charlie to be addressed. I knew he would not care if they just called him Charlie. We discussed that possibility. Maybe it would work.

Upon my daughter's arrival at my house, the next installment of the story surfaced. Since our last phone call, Obadiah had been pushing to call him Grandpa Charlie. At six years old, this child could already debate with the best of us.

"Obadiah bugged me until I finally told him he could call Charlie 'Grandpa Charlie,'" admitted Camelia.

After a time of reveling in his victory, Obadiah dropped the subject. He seemed pleased that his mom had related all the details of their discussion to me.

Then suddenly he said, "No, I think I'd like to call him Chuck." Well, Charlie is just not a Chuck; Chuck is a cowboy. Still, Charlie loved cowboy movies. Maybe...

As soon as Charlie called that week, I told him what the kids would call him. I could almost hear that belly laugh *without* the use of the phone over this new twist to the story.

Another time I heard Obadiah telling someone about his three grandfathers. One was Grandpa So-and-So, another was Grandpa So-and-So, and the third was Charlie. "No, Chuck," he corrected himself. "He lives in a jail." From the look on the woman's face, I do not think she believed that part of the story.

The day came for them all to meet Charlie. My three-and-a-half-foot-tall grandson, after going through all the security, walked up to my six-foot-three husband as bold and confident as he could be. He pushed his hand out to shake Charlie's and said, "Hello, Chuck." We all burst out laughing. It remains one of our fondest memories.

Two of my children did not meet Charlie. The idea of our marriage concerned each of them in different ways and we recognized them in this decision. But there was more to come on this front. Meanwhile, Charlie and I would continue on our trek into the unknown.

Chapter 15

RELATIONSHIP OF HEALING

Being treasured by a man was a new experience for me. Charlie loved me as I was, and we basked in the comfort and joy God gave us day by day. The path we'd chosen wouldn't be easy, but I felt confident that we could make it through the hard times that would certainly come. The question that sometimes bothered me was, could we fight with each other and make it? Could we say hurting things when angry and go beyond to real forgiveness? The prison environment makes it hard to communicate, especially the things that come with a raised voice.

"Charlie, I have to be honest. I have said for years that my lack of trust in men is because I have to trust God more. Not trusting you is a reflection that I don't trust God."

"I know, Dear. It will all be fine because you are honest," he responded.

I certainly tried to be honest, but situations from the past came up occasionally that kept getting in Charlie's and my way.

"I am trying to lose weight," I told him one day. "I want to look good for you."

"I like you the way you are. I am not the slimmest man here," he joked. "How much do you weigh?" Certainly, this was a normal question under the circumstances. I had brought it up.

"Charlie, I hate to tell my weight to anyone," I said, thinking this was honest. Well, it probably was, but it was rather foolish. Charlie recognized my sensitivity and dropped the subject, but my own response bothered me. *What was that about, Lord? I know he loves me.*

From that time, he showed me by action that he truly did accept me how I was. If I wanted to lose weight, he supported me, but he never rejected me or said unkind things when I gained. I was coming to see that he really just accepted me. But that was mild.

When we began corresponding, I thought he had told me in a letter, "I don't do visits and I don't do phone calls." After we got engaged, he mentioned that he had called someone. That seemed strange. I thought he didn't do phone calls. Surely he did not mean that he called other people but did not call me.

With great trepidation, I decided to bring up the subject. "I thought you didn't make phone calls, but you said you called someone, didn't you?"

"I said I don't like phone calls and don't do visits."

"But your letter said you don't do phone calls or visits. That is why I was surprised you wanted me to visit." I could almost picture the words "I do not do phone calls" written in a letter. I kept at it, asking questions as they came to mind.

Finally he glared at me with fire in his eyes. "Get the hell out of here. You are calling me a liar. And don't ever come back."

He stood up and went toward a guard.

For a moment I sat paralyzed. Stunned, I could not think what to do or say. I knew that I was not accusing him of lying. My mind was a total blank; he was telling me once again not to visit. My face flushed red with regret and hidden tears. This felt all too familiar. Anger and accusations. Men indict. Men bully women. They never try to talk it out. Every one of my old mental tapes was replaying furiously as I tried to pin down one rational thought. I could not do it.

Oh God, is this the end of our relationship? I stood to leave. The tapes in my head kept rolling. Were we done? *Why is it that every time I am honest in a relationship, men reject me?* I walked toward the sally port and was escorted to the lobby. I hoped no one could see my hands shaking.

Lord, don't let me cry. Keep me from the embarrassment of tears, please. Help me to hold on to a piece of my dignity. It is enough that the whole room is checking out the disturbance.

I made it to the car without shedding a tear. With so many curves to maneuver as I drove, I even made it to Route One without a drop. Then the dam of my emotions burst. I headed home, but buildings and businesses I had passed many times before whizzed by in a blur. Cars maneuvered around me and me around them, seemingly without my notice.

Lord, why did this happen? You knew it would happen. He would be like the others. I did it again. I chose someone who is a bully. My first marriage was full of false accusations. I cannot do this. You knew, and You could have stopped me. You could have had others stop me. Why? Lord, why?

Gut-wrenching sobs burst forth from a hiding place deep down inside me. Waves of anger, frustration, and rage exploded as if from someone other than myself. I was expressing pain as if it had been held back for many years. I alternately cried and yelled for almost two hours. I finally stopped and called my friend Nanda, asking her to meet me at my house. Never having experienced such dark frustration, I was going off the deep end into sheer panic. I desperately needed help.

On the trip home I tried to imagine what Charlie was thinking. I knew he would get over being upset with me, but would he ever want to see me again? I couldn't say. All I could think was why, why, why?

Soon after I got home, Nanda arrived to talk and pray with me. My sighs from prolonged weeping retreated as she walked in and hugged me. Then my phone rang, and it was another friend.

"Kay, I was hoping you would not answer the phone. I wanted to tell you this on your message machine. I do not want to be in the middle of this. But here it is. Charlie and Mike called, and Charlie wants to know if you will forgive him for what he did today. I really do not want to be doing this. He is paying for the calls. And he will call my house again at 8 p.m. to see what you say."

"Of course I forgive him. If I come over to your house by eight, could I talk to him?" I had a cell phone, not a landline, and at the time the prison phones could not do the complicated process to listen in on calls on a cell phone. I had no idea what the rules on the phone were, but I wanted to talk to Charlie. My heart soared that he had done what was right and asked forgiveness for yelling at me and sending me home.

Plans were made to go to my friend's house later that night. When Mike called, she asked him to hand the phone to Charlie as she handed me her phone. What a blessing to hear his voice on the phone for the first time ever.

"Hi, Sweetheart," I said.

"Who is this?" He was not at all expecting me to be there.

"It's Kay. And of course I forgive you. Will you forgive me for badgering you?"

After he got over the shock of me being on the other end of the line, we forgave each other. Sorting it all out would come when I could see him face-to-face. The whole incident by itself was a milestone for me and for us. A man had actually asked forgiveness from me and meant it, a first in my life. But more was coming.

I also got this in a letter he wrote that afternoon: "Hi, Honey, well, it's me, Mr. Ugly. Aren't I just the one? Can't let go of some things. But I am trying. Sorry that I got upset at visits today. It's the only time we have together each week, and I go and get upset over stupid things. I am sorry, Honey. Forgive me."

I forgave, but still a small place in my heart voiced a need to find out exactly what he had written in his letter long ago. In going over my letters, I found the one I wanted and discovered I had been wrong. He had actually said that he did not do visits and did not *like* phone calls. I wrote him immediately to ask his forgiveness.

I realized that the Lord was teaching us how to handle disagreement. We would somehow work out the differences; it was extreme for him to kick me out of there, and it was extreme for me to worry so much about a few words. I needed to trust him to have other people in his life. He needed to trust me not to be calling him a liar. Trust issues. Learning about real love is a difficult process.

At church, I was still upset. "Bernadette, can you pray with me?" I asked another friend.

"Sure, what happened?"

"Oh, Charlie exploded at me, but we got it straightened out. I am still down in the dumps, though," I said.

After a moment of prayer she said, "Kay, this is all about your first marriage. This is not about Charlie. This is NOT about Charlie."

"Oh, my goodness, it is not about Charlie!" I knew instantly that this was a revelation from God. My heart soared as she continued to pray for us both.

With her words, all the gears meshed into place and clicked, grinding to a fast halt. I realized the truth. I had never grieved the failed marriage nor expressed my anger over it. Years of unresolved feelings had piled up, and the overflow was spilling out all over my precious Charlie.

In fact, I was grieving all that had happened in my life that I had not grieved. I had ignored and suppressed disappointment all my life. I finally had moved into pretending that I had no desire for a deep, abiding relationship with a man. Yes, I was angry about the marriage in my past, but I was also angry that I had been told not to cry, not to ever grieve the simple desires I had for companionship with a boy in my teen years or a man in my adult years. I had been told at seventeen in effect not to seek the otherliness of a man. During the years since my divorce, people had said to me that it was strange I never got angry about my first marriage. It was strange and more. At last exposing my anger to the Lord after all these years was like a refreshing shower, finally bringing my soul into healing light through an incident with this loving man. I forgave my ex-husband, this time from my heart. Not only was I enjoying a sense of cleansing, I was learning that Charlie and I could have a fight and get beyond it. Two big miracles. God's timing is always perfect. We had learned how to get through a fight before we ever got married. And it was just three months until the wedding.

Chapter 16

A NORMAL WEDDING?

Well, God is working on us," Charlie remarked when we saw each other again.

"I know. What a revelation I had over this. In my past with men, I cannot remember a time when someone really asked me for forgiveness...I treasure you, Charlie." My hand reached out to caress his. He flashed a now familiar silly smile, eyes crossed.

"I want our marriage to be as normal as it can be," I added.

"It will be if we let God do it for us. We just don't have the answers," Charlie said. "He always points me to Jesus when things are rough, saying 'God is with us.' God Emmanuel."

I smiled.

"You know, Kay, I may never get out of this place."

I nodded, but my eyes drifted away. We had talked about it as a possibility, but now it seemed unlikely he would receive clemency before our wedding date. The process takes months if it ever gets moving. The first step is to get the Clemency Board to allow it to go to the governor. And most governors do not want to deal with this part of their job.

"People want to know now how this is going to work, and I don't know. I have no idea how it will all work out, Charlie."

"I know. Me either. We only have today. I think something will happen sometime, but we don't know when."

With that in mind, we asked the Lord to show us how we could have a wedding. God's next lesson came when a retired missionary friend from Maryland happened to call. He had been in Iraq with me and had gently teased me about marriage.

After a brief "Hello," Manny joked, "So did you get married yet?" He always asked, but I don't think he was expecting this response:

"No," I replied, "but I will be soon."

"Tell me all about him! I want to share it with the rest of our team." I knew he loved to call everyone and report any big news about our team from Erbil. So much had happened to us all, and we had grown close in that hard place. Manny was the glue that kept us together after we left.

How do you explain marriage to someone in prison in a few words on the phone or a few lines on paper? My hearing loss made it even more difficult by phone. "Manny, I promise I will tell you about Charlie, but it will be on paper if you don't mind. Then you can call everyone and tell them about it."

As I wrote out my answer to him, it was like telling a story. Manny was a dear friend, so I knew he would accept the situation for what it was.

Manny called as soon as he got my letter and said, "You sure know how to shock a fellow. I can't get over it. Are you happy?" Leave it to Manny to ask the right question.

"I am, and I love this man so much." What else could I say?

Manny and his dear wife sent along a generous gift of money for us, showing their support. What a delightful surprise that was! It gave me hope that other people would accept this next step in our lives.

Being a missionary, I have people who support me in prayer and also in finances. I knew my supporters deserved to know about our upcoming marriage quickly and not hear it from others. How could I tell them? Then it hit me.

I took the letter to Manny and wrote a more general version for my next newsletter. A multitude of counselors for this change in direction in my life was in order, and my supporters had all walked with me through many toils and trials over the years. I couldn't predict how they would respond. I just had to trust God.

People had no idea what to say at first. As Manny had said, it was a shock. But God knew all this and prepared us as best as anyone could be prepared for the unknown.

What is normal anyway? What is a normal marriage celebration? What alternatives did we have?

Your ways are not our ways. But maybe You have a way to plan for our marriage celebration that will be similar to what a more "normal" marriage is.

Charlie was asking official questions on his end. The prison would not allow us to have cake or punch for the wedding, or flowers. We could have one friend each to witness this marriage.

Charlie wanted Tiny to be his best man, but the reception would have to occur elsewhere. Carrie Sue would be my matron of honor. I wished more of our friends and family could be there. But I needed to be thankful for what we had. Some prisons would not even allow us to marry. It was, after all, a prison.

"Honey, I don't think I'll get a cut in my sentence," Charlie began one day. "You may as well organize a reception at the house. We'll figure something." Oh, how I wanted Charlie to be part of everything! *How do we have a reception, Lord? Do we wait and see if You will let him out? Charlie said to just go ahead with one at home.* I couldn't imagine doing a reception if the groom could not attend. That is why it is called a reception. People would be receiving the couple as the two have become one. Being received as a couple by the body of Christ was significant to us. It was also vital for us to acknowledge and receive others as our family of support. They would hold us accountable to our vows.

Charlie had to be part of the reception at home without being there; I wanted to be part of whatever was going on at the prison.

"What exactly do we want for our reception?" I asked one day at our visit.

"What do you mean?"

"Well, what is important to you?"

"I can't come, so what does it matter?"

"It does. For instance, would you want a sit-down dinner if you could come?"

"No," he answered. I could almost hear him wondering why I was asking.

"I don't want to throw a bouquet either, especially since I cannot have one at the wedding. I love flowers, but don't want that. I can easily get rid of a lot of these traditions." I added, "I would like our brothers and sisters to be able to pray over us."

"That would be nice. What are you thinking?"

"Well, we could save up for the phone and somehow do it by phone," I said.

A change in prison policy had occurred, allowing Charlie to call my cell phone. My cell phone was actually the first one to be on the prison line. The prison had caught up with the times, recognizing they needed to provide for cell phone use. Another small piece of God's plan! After a few tries, Charlie and I had been able to talk on the phone once a week. As we prayed about the reception, a strategy formed. Charlie could call at the time of the function; I would talk and then ask who else wanted to meet Charlie by phone. They could pray with us too. I suspected there would be some sort of merriment for Charlie back in his pod.

We were now looking at having two separate receptions with a bridge by phone for prayer. We might not be able to kiss when forks hit the glasses, but we would enjoy being with friends in person and on the phone.

Seeing now that we just needed to sort out what was important, I came up with a simple solution for invitations. I would just write out what was really happening. Family and friends would join us on our journey, by prayer, and then the reception would be after this.

Charles Wilbur Page and
Katherine Mary Winkler
request the honor of your presence in prayer
from your home for their wedding on Saturday,
September 3, 2005 at
Maine State Prison

❧

We regret that you cannot attend the ceremony in person.
Please join us in prayer at 12 noon.
After the ceremony, Charlie and Kay will visit each other and
then return to their respective homes.

❧

You are invited to a reception at Kay's house at 6 p.m.

Our plans solidified. On our wedding day I would go up and visit in the morning and be wed at noon. Our honeymoon would be our usual afternoon visit.

"Charlie, I will travel back home after our honeymoon visit in the afternoon. I can be there for a reception at 6 p.m. You call at six, and I will pass the phone around so people can talk to you or pray for us."

"Okay. I like that idea," he said. "It costs $1.80 each time we hook up and then $.25 for each minute. What about that?"

"We can both save up the money to put into the prepay call account," I answered. "If there is a lockdown, then call back after if you can."

"Yeah, what about a lockdown? You will have to explain about that," he urged me.

"I will explain just how important it is to hand the phone to me if that happens." The man says lockdown, you lock down. We knew all kinds of things could happen, but we were happy. Our plans were coming together.

Chapter 17

CLOTHES AND RINGS AND BLACK INK

T he invitations went out for our wedding, and hope rose up in our hearts. The most difficult thought was that we could plan and plan, but there still might be a lockdown at the time for the wedding. It was another "trust the Lord place" in our lives. If that happened, then the plans would have to move to the next available time for the ceremony.

"God will be right there with us, no matter what happens, Dear," Charlie assured me.

"I am going to start searching thrift shops for something to wear, Charlie," I said.

"You are going to wear new clothes, so how much money do you need to do that?"

He sent money right away, and then my sister got involved. She knew places to shop for everything I wanted, and she also contributed money to dress up her sister properly for this joyous event. Kerry and I stomped the streets of Boston, searching shops that were not too high-priced and had things I liked. It was a toss-up which one of us was more excited.

At another visit I pondered, "Charlie, we have to size our rings. I wonder how we do that for you."

"Well, I asked the prison if I could step out for a few days to have it done in Sanford, but they said it was not possible," he joked.

"If the groom can't come by the store, how could we size our rings?" I asked at a jewelry shop. They said I could borrow the sizer and bring it back in a few days.

My next trip up to the prison, I asked how I could bring in a sizer to have Charlie's ring size done. I knew it would be considered contraband if I just brought the sizer. They had to know everything beforehand. First I had to get permission from the sergeant in charge of visit room security.

"You bring it to the lobby and the rover will carry it down to the visit room. Charlie will try them on and decide what size he needs," the sergeant explained. "You will hand the sizer to the rover and he will bring it back to the lobby. Then you will collect the sizer at the desk. Don't forget to schedule it with the visit person."

Thinking out loud about the rigmarole, I told Carrie Sue that I needed a ring sizer and she said she had one. Surely she was joking! But no, she really had a ring sizer. After all, don't we all have one in the kitchen drawer? I needed that laugh.

"I am buying the rings," Charlie insisted.

It was no passing trifle for Charlie to make such a commitment, since it takes many hours of real labor for an inmate to save up that much money. He is paid well as prisons go at $1.70 an hour. But because he's often been sick, he has lost time on the job. Buying our rings was truly a labor of love.

I went looking. I found the perfect matching rings, with comfort edges for us old folks.

"What Scripture do you want inside our rings?" I asked. We wanted something personal and significant on both. Charlie picked out a verse from the Song of Songs.

Every little thing that we on the outside take for granted is a major procedure inside the prison. But sometimes God, with an amazing sense of humor, makes it fun rather than a chore. The marriage license was another hurdle. I told Charlie I would go get it soon.

"Okay. I will see if I can get a day off from work to come with you," he said with that twinkle in his eye.

I called the Sanford town office to see what information I needed and what process I would have to go through to get the license. They gave me the details. Because Charlie and I had been married before, we needed verification of the dates of both our divorces. Those papers were in the archives. I was not afraid to tell people I was marrying someone in prison, but only if it was an essential part of the story. It usually saved time. I was not in the least ashamed of the wonderful partner God had chosen for me. But I could see shock in people's faces. After all, they knew only what they saw on TV each year, literally thousands of rapes and murders, and no changed lives.

The gal who waited on me at the town hall was very efficient and rather stone-faced, and she had me do all sorts of things to fill out papers. Finally she said the groom would have to come with me for the next step.

"What if he cannot come here?"

"Well, he has to come," she said.

"He can't," I replied.

"Why?"

"He is in prison."

There came a long, heavy pause as she took in that information, and then droning on, she told me what he had to do to fill out her form. She mentioned that it had to be done in black ink as well as notarized.

In my next letter I said, "Charlie, you need to fill out this part and this part. It has to be notarized and filled out in black ink."

My thought was that notarizing would be another hurdle. I was wrong. They have someone on staff come to the visit room and notarize on the spot. Of course it is logical to have that with so many legal dealings inside the walls.

Alas, no detail is a small detail when dealing with prisons. Our application came back from Charlie filled out in blue with his explanation that he could not have a black pen. Black pens are for official prison documents, and no inmate could have them.

Back again to the town office. I heard a flurry of voices and then ducked heads all apparently relating that this was the lady marrying someone from prison.

Immediately the woman who had taken care of me earlier came over to help. With a deadpan look that only she could do, she said, "This has to be filled out with black ink. It says so right here on the application," she added, pointing so I could see where I had made my mistake.

"My fiancé cannot get a black pen. The prison does not allow a prisoner to have a black pen." From the look on her face, I could tell she doubted this. So I waited.

Lord, I do wonder at some of the restrictions. Thank You for this unusual man You have given me. I took a minute to just praise God for all He was doing. The woman was in real agony, knowing my situation and apparently knowing her situation with rules. Pondering it for what seemed like an hour, she finally said that the blue pen on our application would be okay.

"But," she explained further, "on the real marriage license application that your officiate will have to fill out after the wedding is done, it *must* be done in black. It has to go to the secretary of state." My mind went to thinking how much fun a humorist would have with this story. Tim Sample, look out. I assured her that Ray would bring a black ink pen. I hoped it would not be a problem for the prison. From that point on, my pastor kept a note attached to his wedding plans folder that said, "Bring a black ink pen." I actually had no idea what the prison would and would not allow to come in with the pastor who would marry us.

Clothes bought, licenses taken care of, and invitations sent, Charlie and I could relax and continue to plan what we wanted to do for fun.

"I ordered lots of pictures for the wedding," Charlie told me. "The money goes to the Inmate Benefit Fund."

I soon met the photographer, another inmate. Each visit he came in and set up a colorful canvas background for the pictures. This was his first wedding assignment, and he kept asking, "Do you want your pictures this week?" Just because the wedding was scheduled for a certain date did not mean it would happen then. Maybe that was why he checked so often. Or maybe he was excited to have a wedding to photograph. He would be able to take candid shots not allowed in the "Here we stand before the painted picture glued to the floor" kind of pictures he usually did.

"I will get pictures of the Sanford reception taken so you can see who was at the party." Charlie looked pleased. I had a card-making program on my computer, so I was able to keep him up on whatever was going on at home by making note cards with pictures to use for my daily letters. I often thought at times like this, *It is such a simple task for me, and yet he appreciates these details.*

People in prison are allowed to keep only a certain number of pictures. If he got a new one that he wanted to keep, he had to get rid of another picture. He would have plenty from which to choose. The only thing we could not capture in pictures would be the festivity at Charlie's pod.

Ray came up another time to talk about the service itself. "We cannot have communion, but we would like it if we could have some fellowship time. We don't want to hurry anything." One of the key things we wanted was to have as much time for fellowship as we were allowed. I wanted everyone to get to know each other. Charlie could get to know Ray and Carrie Sue a little more. All of us from outside wanted to get to know the best man, Tiny, better. Charlie and I wanted to be able to walk around the room holding hands, something we could not do at visits. Simple things, but they were important in our planning.

"That's easy," Ray said when he heard all my hopes.

"How?" I replied.

"We just have to have a fellowship time during the service," he smiled.

Fellowship time at River of Life is a time set aside to practice the "fellowship of the saints." An important part of our journey with the Lord is to be with our brothers and sisters, just living life. This is called fellowship. It is hard to imagine getting married to someone with whom you have only been seated across a table, someone with whom you've never had coffee nor eaten a meal and hardly ever walked with holding hands except a short trip up to get pictures taken at a regular visit. But we hoped we could at least walk around to say hello to the participants.

Charlie inquired, but security would not allow communion. Charlie could receive communion at his church service, but we could not have it at our wedding. It was *the* major disappointment for us in all this.

My friend Carrie Sue was allowed to be at the wedding, but there were others who walked with me through our unusual circumstances, praying and counseling me along our journey. Nanda was going with me to the prison on our wedding day, even though she would not be allowed to be inside the visit room for the wedding. "Why don't you and Carrie

Sue and I go to a motel near the prison the night before the ceremony?" she suggested. "That way you don't have to drive the long trip just before the wedding."

"That is perfect," I replied. "I also know I will need your support as the time gets near. Thanks."

Being an older bride does not eliminate all of the jitters. So I stopped by a local place in Warren and made arrangements for us ladies to stay the night of September second. My friend Pat, Ray's wife, was also coming on the day of the wedding. She would have to wait outside in the lobby too. She would be company for Nanda.

Arrangements for the reception were being made by a few ladies from the church, my friends. Sherry worked at The Shed doing a Maine version of the Sonshine Club. She knew her way around my house. Priscilla was full of wedding ideas and also wanted to help.

Blessing me to no end, they both were excellent at organization, not my strong suit. I only had to think about the details they wanted me to be in on, such as color schemes and cake choices. They planned food, decorations, and how to fit lots of people into The Shed. We even had awnings in case it rained that day.

The body of Christ is a family, and we could not have done it without our large extended family, both inside the walls and outside on the street. River of Life took the lead for us at home, while Tiny took the lead inside the prison. I am sure I will not know everyone who helped until I get to heaven. But we were so grateful to them all.

Charlie and I had talked about the neighborhood where I lived and worked. We had to plan for a sudden release in case the clemency bid came through. If he came home, then our neighbors would all have a new neighbor just out of prison, one who had been in prison for murder. Therefore, my final preparation for the wedding was delivering invitations by hand to the neighbors. I wanted to make sure they were aware of Charlie, in case they had questions. Our desire was to remain as open as possible about the circumstances of our life together. We loved and respected the honesty in each other, and we wanted to make that a hallmark of our lives as a couple. We also wanted the neighbors to come to the celebration.

One woman in her late seventies asked me point-blank, "Aren't you afraid he will kill you?"

"No, he's like Santa Claus." Charlie and I had a good chuckle over that one.

Taking invitations to the people I knew, I told them about the wedding, which they were all aware of anyway. News travels fast in our little community. Now the neighbors were joined into our family, celebrating our union under God.

I was to find out after this that many more people in the neighborhood loved the fact that I was married to someone in prison. Several of them had had the terrible experience of being in prison or loving someone inside the walls. I suspected that was one of the reasons the Lord had relocated me here. God was on the move.

Chapter 18

THE WEDDING

T he night before the wedding, Nanda, Carrie Sue, and I checked into our motel and went off to Moody's Diner for supper. It's a true 1950s diner with old-fashioned booths that really are old, not just reproductions. Most restaurants in Maine serve lobster and steak, but not Moody's. They specialize in "home cooking"—meatloaf, hot dogs, beef stew, burgers, brown beans, and possibly the finest lemon meringue pie on earth. They might have a lobster roll, but mostly it's food like Mom cooked.

Returning to the motel room, we did what girls do. Every detail of how I would dress, what I would wear for earrings, and how I would do my hair was planned out. We chattered, joked, and prayed for two more hours. When I took out my hearing aids, I soon fell off to sleep, not at all bothered by my friends' continuing chatter.

My wedding day began with the free "continental breakfast" offered by the motel, consisting of store-bought doughnuts in cellophane, over-cooked coffee, and powdered creamer. In a friendly conversation, the proprietor asked, "So what are you ladies doing for the day?"

Nanda said, "We are all going to a wedding." No one mentioned the whereabouts of the event since we knew he might be shocked. We all three managed to keep a straight face. Our festive mood was not going to be stopped. Giggling as we left, my friends began saying. "Where are we going? Where are we going?"

"We are going to the prison for my wedding," I managed to say before going into more fits of laughter.

Back to the room for the final decisions about luggage, hair acces-sories, and gathering of clothes to take, and then we were off. *Get me to the prison on time. If I am dancing...*

Sailing down the final stretch of road to the prison, we spotted a yard sale. Carrie Sue and I had gone to lots of yard sales during our years of friendship. She glanced at me and said, with merriment in her eyes, "Wanna go in?" Without missing a beat or waiting for an answer, she turned the car into the driveway, and the three of us laughed harder at the absurdity of going into a yard sale on the way to your own wedding. Now that is devotion to bargains!

Quicker than my cat can escape out the door, I can zip my eyes across everything in a yard sale. I looked. Of course, I was not going to really buy anything. But I could not resist going over and checking the tables, even on this eventful day. On one table was a white pillow that caught my eye. I wanted it, but hesitated. I did not want to make us late.

We drove the final mile to the prison. The ladies brought me to the lobby door and then parked the car for the next stage of the adventure. I went inside and signed the visit book with my name, address, town, state, and person I would visit. It occurred to me that this would be the last time I would sign in with my old name since I did not have to sign in for the wedding. It was the last time I would visit Charlie before my name changed to his. My friends sat chatting with me until the morning visit was called.

Other visitors who knew I was getting married after this visit wished me well. Good news is always shared inside the walls. Marriage is the stuff of dreams. With me, Nanda and Carrie Sue went over my instructions to them again, very patient with my nerves. "Have my clothes ready. Also a brush for my hair. Did someone bring the rosettes for my hair?" While I was in the morning visit with Charlie, they were going to take the car to explore the area before the noontime wedding. They assured me they would be back at 10:30 and would have my change of clothes there. They truly were ladies in waiting for me, attending to my every desire. I could not think for myself at all by this time. Just random thoughts. If any two people knew my concerns about marriage—about marrying someone the Lord had not chosen and just about marrying at all—it was Carrie Sue and Nanda.

"Make sure you go get a booth in the bathroom as soon as the visit is over," I said. I knew how the booths all filled after each visit, and I wanted enough time just in case we got back in the visit room for the wedding earlier than we expected.

As I waited for visits to be called—the last time for me as a single woman—we went over more and more details. You know I am nervous by how many details I am quizzing people with at the last minute before an event! As soon as I could after our visit, I would head to the ladies' room.

"Visits!" the guard on duty announced. I hugged my friends and thanked them for their support and friendship through my unusual courtship and engagement.

Ray was coming in at ten so we could go over the ceremony details for the last time. It was not like we'd had leisurely days to go over the prison procedures in addition to the usual wedding traditions. It's traditional for the bride to be kept away from the groom until she walks down the aisle on her wedding day. That's one tradition I easily abandoned. I thanked God for this final visit with Charlie before our wedding.

Charlie had his hair newly cut for the wedding and his beard was gleaming white and trimmed. He looked quite striking.

"You look very handsome today," I said.

"You're pretty good-looking yourself," he replied, smiling.

I asked him what he knew about the timing after this visit was over. Would we go right back in, or would they delay it until twelve? He sometimes got snippets of information from a guard who sympathized a bit, really wanting a semblance of decent life for the men inside. But Charlie knew nothing.

We were still gazing into one another's eyes when Ray arrived. "All right you two," he quipped. "Let's get on with it." Ray had been praying about the ceremony, and I wanted to know what the Lord had shown him.

"We know that the details of the vows are going to be perfect, Ray. You are the one with the lifelong marriage. We both failed at that. We know you have wisdom, and we know what we need to promise in here today."

Ray outlined the order of service and the Scriptures he said the Lord had shown him.

"Tiny will be reading something about marriage he has for us," Charlie added. This was a particularly tender offering since Tiny was having trouble in his own marriage. The visit ended as usual, at 10:30 sharp.

To the man inside the walls, time grinds on painfully slowly. Yet he lives by a rigid schedule over which he lacks any control. We had "scheduled" our wedding weeks ago, but prison officials determine when it would actually happen, if at all. Prison weddings are usually set around the guards' lunchtime, but if the guards are occupied with some other business, you just have to wait.

No one would commit to what specific time we would actually go back in, but they assured us they would tell us both when we could go back to the visit room to be married. Again, this was for security reasons. If a lockdown was ordered for some reason, the wedding would be off. Nothing in life is sure, but this was not even close to firm. I could see this wedding was going to be from the Lord and for His glory. In prison, once a decision is made, all the powers that be consistently back it, whether they agree with the decision or not. And it was all in the name of security. I was learning to live one moment at a time. But I could still go to the Lord with my petitions. The Lord wants us to trust Him moment by moment, and I was learning that even on my wedding day.

Lord, let us be able to have our wedding today.

The end of the visit arrived too soon, and Ray left us to embrace once more before the wedding. "I will see you soon, Sweetheart," Charlie whispered loudly in my ear. He knew I needed support, as did he.

"Yes. It will happen."

All this uncertainty was on my mind as I rushed out to the ladies' room to find Carrie Sue and Nanda, ready and waiting in the stall. I changed, and they helped me get my makeup fixed and hair redone, complete with pinning little cloth rosettes in my hair. Sometimes I wonder if the details of a wedding are so furiously fussy to help the bride calm down. In a short time we managed to get me into my wedding clothes and out of the stall. Now I was ready but had to go through the last wait until we were called to the visit room. We walked into the lobby.

Going over to Ray, I asked, "Do you have a black pen?"

"Of course. You only told me about ten times. Would I let you down?" We laughed.

He then walked over to the corrections officer manning the front desk and explained, "I will be taking in a black ink pen. The town office and the secretary of state require the signatures to be in black ink."

Maybe that man was tired. He never even cracked a smile. Everyone was milling around with nervous jokes, since this was the last wait for all of us in a very long process. The shift changed somehow, and a new man came to the lobby desk.

Pat and I talked about how she and Ray were going home after the wedding. They were taking Nanda and Carrie Sue, who had come in my car the night before. I would leave alone.

It is good they are all thinking, I thought again. I had never considered that little detail of getting them back over one hundred miles to home after the wedding! Obviously they would not want to wait until three to go home with me. Besides, they were going to my house to help set up for the reception. Nanda had practically redesigned The Shed for the occasion.

Doing time well became a reality for me right then. With time dragging, I got a bright idea that I would hear about for the rest of my life. I decided it was terrible that Nanda, who had prayed so long, helped plan, and had spent the night up there to help out, could not go see the wedding. She was even going to the reception early in the afternoon, to ensure the setup was what she envisioned. Months before, one of the guards had mentioned that he hoped he could go to the control room to watch Charlie's wedding. He really liked Charlie. Being somewhat of a novice at prison details, I had no idea what the control room was for, since the whole place was about control anyway. But I remembered the term and knew someone could see the wedding from there. I also knew it was a darkened room off the hall we went down when being escorted to the visit room. I had just never put two and two together.

"Could my friend Nanda go to the control room to watch the wedding?" I asked. I knew the officer at the desk and knew he was reasonable. I thought this was a brilliant idea because I remembered we could see monitors through the dark glass surround when we passed the control room. It would be perfect for her.

"Haaaaa!! The control room! She wants her friend to go to the control room!" His lively comeback was startling, to say the least. His loud guffaw drew all eyes to us immediately. *What did I say?*

Debating whether or not to ask another question, I decided we already were the center of some big joke. Obviously, he was struck by the foolishness of my question, and I had no idea why it was so funny.

"Well, can she?" I asked, wondering if he would ever catch his breath long enough to tell me.

"She wants her friend to go to the control room," he managed to get out before again being taken over by laughter.

He finally managed to spit out, "The control room is the most secure place in the *entire* prison, Kay. No, your friend *could not* go there."

"Okay, just asking," I said. Talk about classic comic relief. Hey, what did I know? Later, that guard told Charlie about it and laughed. Then Charlie brought it up to me. He told the other guards as they came back from breaks. Everyone laughed more.

I have never lived that down. Every single time that guard saw me ever after, he said, "She wants her friend to go to the control room," and he laughed anew. Joke on me. Joke on Charlie. Joke on a guard. Telling that story to someone who has been around prisons had become a sure-fire way to lighten up almost any situation.

When our escort at last summoned us to the visit room, Ray, Carrie Sue, and I walked through the metal detectors, down the now familiar cinder-block hall, by the windows with only enough yard showing to reveal the razor wire outside, and past the dark glass of the control room to the sally port. We stopped to wait for the doors to open and close on the hall side and then open and close to the room side. I have two vivid memories of walking through a sally port. The first was when I walked through to meet Charlie. This is the second. But this time I was not wondering how I would know him.

There he was, my beloved, my friend, my soon-to-be husband. My eyes were captured by his look alone, and all the people in the room faded to the background. His arms reached out to draw me in and comfort me. Wonder of wonders, we did not have to sit down immediately across the table from each other. Miracle of miracles, we could walk together and talk to each other, holding hands, kissing. The closeness of Charlie was an overwhelming perfume, and I did not care that we were under guard or being watched. Joy filled my heart as I held his arm.

Ray took over, sensing how nervous we still were. I hugged him and then Tiny. We said hello to the photographer and proceeded with introductions and hugs all around.

Charlie and I weren't joking around like usual. This was a somber moment; both of us knew the magnitude of this step. Every marriage has problems. Ours would have even more because of Charlie's incarceration and my decision to join him in doing time until he could leave. Our desire was to please God, but was this realistic? Even though we were sure God wanted our marriage, truthfully, last-minute thoughts were flying like butterflies.

"Lets begin," said Ray, sending a hush through the room. My heart fluttered once, then settled when I looked into Charlie's eyes. He winked and followed it with a slight smile, a fond gesture very familiar to me by now. And I knew this was the most entirely right thing I would ever do in my life. Suddenly, neither of us was aware of other people at all, basking in each other's sight, content to trust God as we listened to the charges Pastor Ray made.

Our witnesses watched as we promised to love, honor, and cherish each other. Finally, putting on wedding rings brought us to the commitment, the actual exchange of vows. We promised until death do us part. Tiny would instruct on marriage.

One of the most precious memories was witnessing the kindness of my husband. He was gentle toward me, of course. But he also was particularly kind toward Tiny. Tiny was so nervous and concerned with the gravity of our promises, caring so much that we would make it. He had written out a lovely piece about marriage. He choked back tears all the way through the reading.

"Come on. You can do it. That's it. Yes." Charlie encouraged him every single step.

Tiny was speaking truth into our lives: how we were to care for each other forever. As he spoke, no one mentioned the sadness of his own marriage. In fact, that is a cornerstone of those in prison. There often does not seem to be a lot of mention of emotions. People at first reason that this is because there are no emotions; if one has done something to deserve prison, surely he is hardened too much to have them. What is really going on is that if you know the feelings a fellow inmate is having, you keep it to yourself and support your friend. Tiny wanted for Charlie what he did not have in his own life.

Tiny admonished us with Scripture: "For this reason a man shall leave his father and mother and be joined to his wife, and the two shall become one flesh. This is now bone of my bones and flesh of my flesh. Two are better than one. If they fall, one will lift up his companion. Live joyfully with the wife whom you love all the days of your life which He has given you."

I was reminded that Tiny was laying down his life for a friend. *What a good friend You have given my husband, Lord God. What a precious and kindhearted man You have given me. Charlie is soft and yet so strong to stand for his friend who is bringing sober instruction.*

It was over. We were married at last under the direction of the Lord, who had brought us together. "Come on, Honey," Charlie said as he grabbed my hand and walked with me to talk to someone.

"Well, do you have all the pictures you want?" I asked the photographer. He had been shooting us from the time we arrived and now motioned to us to pose for another shot he had dreamed up. He was taking some good, professional shots for us.

There are photos of me leaning on Charlie, because I cannot do that at visits. Just resting my head on his chest; what bewildering pleasure that was. And yet, as we stood together, talking to someone else, his arms went around my shoulder as naturally as if we had been married for countless years. We were one now, and we talked together to the others. Such small things were immensely significant. When you only hold hands across a table for most of your time together, each extra-sweet miniature moment becomes a time to savor.

Someone had advised us how long we could stay there. We had to leave the room before the rover for afternoon visits would bring others to the room. This was a gift, to know how long we had left. I desperately did not want to hear "Wedding over" shouted in the tone of a direct order.

At the appropriate instant, just before we knew we must wrap things up, Ray announced that we would have the final prayer. Next he said, "Everybody come and sign in black." We had a hard time keeping a straight face at that direction!

Everyone, including some guards, offered best wishes. We kissed and parted on Ray's direction, not at the bark of a guard. I left the room through one door and Charlie through another. A bit like leaving Wonderland.

In the lobby, Pat, Nanda, Ray, and Carrie Sue waited to hug me and offer their best wishes. As I signed in as Kay Page for the afternoon visit, good-byes were said and my wedding party left.

Now sitting with the other wives and girlfriends, I again received well wishes from them as well as from more guards I knew. One woman came over and practically yelled, "Kay, wasn't today the day you were to get married?" I think I radiated yes, without words.

Along with their excitement, other wives knew better than me that surely there would be great difficulties ahead. I recalled one friend who had met her fiancé on the outside and had been visiting him for eight years at the time we talked. She said, "If I had known how hard it would be, I might not have done it."

This thorny road was somehow made easier in the unique friendships we had because we loved someone on the inside. The festivities had begun, but reminders were everywhere, in every piece of barbed wire, solid brick wall, and metal detector, that this would not be easy.

I still had my afternoon visit with Charlie ahead. It would be our first honeymoon. If the Lord allowed, we wanted someday to have a second honeymoon outside the walls. A friend had even offered his camp for that purpose.

As I reached the visit room for the third time that day, the calm after the turmoil of emotions came as I kissed my husband and felt his arms around me once more. A comfortable place. We had reached the turning point in our life together.

In Charlie's world, there had already been rejoicing with other inmates. "Everyone wanted to buy me a hamburger or something. They were all so happy for me," he said as we sat down. For the inmates, a hamburger was an expensive gift to give.

In our world of the visit room, all our friends were in high spirits for us. Often women who love a person in prison feel compelled to hide the joy from those outside. Here in the visit room, there was no need for anyone to hide their delight. We bonded more deeply in the unique sisterhood of loving a person inside.

Charlie and I started our private life together by praying and thanking the Lord for all He was doing. Our visits had a pattern, due to the constraint of time. We would first go over necessary details of our lives and then settle to pray and/or breathe in each other's company. This day we reviewed the plans for the reception. He would call at six, and others could talk or pray with us. He reminded me to tell everyone about lockdown. Charlie being sent to segregation because of a delay hanging up the phone would certainly not do.

"So how are you doing, Mrs. Page?" Charlie and I took great pleasure in calling each other wife and husband, giggling like two kids.

"Just fine, Mr. Page. I just wish we could get away for a real honeymoon." He gave another soft wink and his secret smile.

Though we would not be together on our wedding night, this moment was tender because we knew each other's pain. Finding the man God had planned for me had been long in coming—more than thirty years. With inexpressible sadness, I left my husband for the first time, to drive to my home hours and miles away from him.

Nanda and Carrie Sue had left my keys at the counter for me to pick up.

I grabbed them on the way out among more congratulations from the visitors and the guards who had just come on duty.

My thoughts were all over the place as I walked to my car. Our life together had been so constricted by time and space that my thoughts exploded. *I have never had a meal with him or driven in the same car. Having a cup of coffee together, is that too much to ask?* Except within the bleak prison walls, I had never been with him in any room at all. How could I return to our home without him?

When I got to the car, there was a gift and a card from Nanda and Carrie Sue waiting for me. A lovely white pillow—the one from the yard sale!

Lord, what a special gift. You planned this so I could laugh right now. It is so hard to leave the very place where my beloved lives. Bless Carrie Sue and Nanda.

Reason kicked in to bring peace to my plummeting feelings. I could look forward to all the firsts ahead, or I could fall rapidly into fear of what was to come. My heart calmed as I chose to seek the Lord's comfort, still wondering when all these firsts would take place, but gratefully aware that we had been able to become one. It was rather like appreciating one M&M rather than chomping on a whole mouthful. I would savor the sweetness of each first in our lives.

Chapter 19

OUR AMAZING RECEPTION(S)

The drive to and from the prison had almost always been a pleasure for me. I got to spend quality time whispering to the Lord and worshiping Him, and sometimes even yelling at Him. His comfort was real on this particular trip home. His wisdom was needed, and the joy of His presence was phenomenal. Since this was the longest day Charlie and I had ever spent together, I had a lot to think about as I drove home. My heart was full for the afternoon ride.

As I drove the final few minutes of the journey home, I could see my house ahead and neighborhood kids gathered at the end of one driveway. Drawing closer, I spotted a tall arbor covered with greens and flowers glowing in the afternoon sun. Several children from the Sonshine Club began jumping up and down, screaming something. Others were clinging to the arbor as I arrived—reminding me of sailors climbing on the rigging of a ship as they spied people on shore. They were yelling, "She's here! Miss Kay is here!" I had to shoo a few of them away from the other driveway so I could park, but I didn't mind. Who could ask for a more joyful greeting?

"Miss Kay. Miss Kay. Take my hand. You have to walk through here!" they yelled as they pulled me through the arbor. "See how pretty it is? See those flowers? I put them in." Another one said, "Do you like the flowers I put on, Miss Kay?"

I smiled, but my mind was drifting to my own children and grandchildren. Sadly, most of them were unable to attend the reception. My son Todd would be coming. I could not let the ache of the others get me down. They lived so far away.

From the moment I arrived, my small group leader, Seth, was snapping pictures, capturing everything that happened that afternoon. Later the gift of all those pictures on a CD was a treasure for me and Charlie. I managed to send some pictures on cards I had made to Charlie later on.

I went into The Shed to see what was going on. The place looked like a fairyland—all swags and twinkling lights. Nanda's vision for the decorations had become a delightful reality thanks to the efforts of Sherry, Jennifer, and the Sonshine Club kids. They worked all the time we were in Warren participating in the wedding ceremony. Another friend had baked and decorated the cake with daisies, one of my favorite flowers. I watched as a couple of helpers did the last-minute work on this piece of art. The aroma of other food was filling the hangout—a hint of things to come.

Cars jammed the narrow street by my house, forcing some to park two streets over. Guests had been arriving all afternoon, not observing the formal arrival time. People were filling the house, The Shed, and the driveway, helping with every detail. Up until this time I'd had no idea if people would shun us or join us. It occurred to me they were ignoring the convention of arriving for a wedding at an exact time because they were just so excited about our unconventional celebration. Each and every new arrival was cause for me to praise God. I was actually surprised that so many cared. I'd known a few people were thrilled, but I had no idea there would be this many here. Happily for all, the organizers had asked lots of people to bring food, so there was plenty to eat, and the old-fashioned washtub filled with ice was bulging with soda cans and water bottles.

As the minutes ticked toward six, I anticipated Charlie's call. Would he get through? I already knew calls from the prisons were an uncertain thing. Lockdown, poorly running equipment, or an unpredictable guard could all contribute to the call not coming. I figured whoever had come was at least okay with the idea of my marrying Charlie. But now would they get to talk to him? All the unknowns were teaching me trust.

My phone rang. Pushing 0 to receive the call, I heard, "Your call has gone through."

"Hi, Sweetheart. How are you?" I said to let Charlie know I had answered the phone.

"Hi there," came the familiar reply. I could picture him winking. The pain of not being together on our wedding night flew through my head, but I would not entertain the beastly thoughts. I was so relieved to hear his voice. God was truly in charge and had arranged for this melding of our receptions.

"I'm good," he continued. I could hear the merriment in the background. I told him I loved him.

The first person up when I asked who wanted to talk was Todd, my son. Accordingly I said to Charlie, "I want you to meet my son Todd." Todd went on to put in an application to visit Charlie and subsequently met him in person. But their talking was blessing enough for me that day.

We had planned to continue the conversation as long as Charlie could stay near the phone and there was not a lockdown. Gradually lots of people at the reception had a chance to talk to him. Everyone was thoughtful of each other and did not stay on the phone too long.

A particular joy and surprise for us both was the fact that many of the men and women who served in Kairos outside the walls were there. Several had to travel quite a distance. It was so extraordinary to Charlie that people he knew would come all this way to pray with him and be with me.

Many of the kids from The Shed wanted to say hello. Friends and loved ones from out of town as well as in town came to wish us well and pray. It was tremendous.

One long-time friend and her husband came. I had actually been prayer partners with her when she was being courted by her husband many years before. Her husband got the phone first and prayed for Charlie and me. Then she said she wanted to pray with Charlie.

I handed her the phone, and tears came to her eyes. She stood for a moment and could say nothing. Then she just sobbed, "Oh, Charlie, I can't say anything. I am so overwhelmed by what the Lord is doing with you both." And she cried some more and then said good-bye. That was the whole conversation. It was a sweet moment for both Charlie and me.

Glory to You, dear Lord, that our friends share in our joy. So many are helping us begin this uncharted path. Thank You. We truly do not walk alone. You have sent Your people.

The phone call went on for what seemed like ages as others continued to talk to Charlie. Later he told me, "I can't believe how many people talked to me. I didn't know how many Christians were out there. I never imagined that there could be so many who cared enough to come and to pray."

Neither did I. His response was a bittersweet reminder of how shut off from the world people inside the walls are. It was a surprise to both of us how many approved of our marriage. I knew some along the way had registered disapproval.

Finally, it happened. Charlie got a lockdown call. He told the man speaking to him to give me the phone. Charlie said good-bye to me and hung up. I told everyone what had happened. The Lord was showing my friends some of the harsh realities of prison life.

But it was not long before the phone rang again. Lockdown was over and Charlie called back. This time I could hear more noise than usual. The guys inside were celebrating. I could hear part of his reception, and he could hear part of mine. In Warren the guys were determined not to let the earlier lockdown spoil their celebration.

I finally had to say good-bye to my new husband. But we had a treasure to keep in our hearts. Though we were more than a hundred miles apart, our receptions had blended into one event—a sweet fellowship with close friends.

Love cannot be blocked by the walls of a prison. I went to bed that night a very content woman, awestruck by the Lord's plan.

Chapter 20

THE STORYTELLER

N o one enjoyed a good story—or told one—like Charlie. His quick wit and raucous laugh regularly broke through the dark cloud of gloom that hovers over the Maine State Prison. Just watching him laugh was an event. First there was an explosion of noise, followed by a loud blast when he emptied his lungs. Out of nowhere his long arms would shoot up behind him, and he would rock so far in his chair that I feared he would crash to the floor backward. All the while, the volume of his guffaws would increase as he pondered the joke more. I think Charlie invented the belly laugh.

Many times everyone in the visit room would discreetly keep peeking as we roared together at some random remark he made. For example, there were often announcements about various meetings and codes that came over a loudspeaker as we talked. One day, one came over the intercom announcing that the AA meeting was starting somewhere. The loudspeaker was extremely loud and irritating even for me. Charlie remarked just as loudly, "Thanks for letting me know." Quickly Charlie flashed a wry smile, and others started laughing with us.

One of Charlie's favorite stories began with a trip to Portland for an eye exam related to his diabetes. I'll never forget him telling it.

"They never tell you exactly when or where you're going. On that day, a guard told me early in the morning to get dressed to travel. I wear an orange shirt and pants when out of the prison. The shirt has the name of the prison on the back in case I get lost," he grinned.

"The guards finish 'dressing me' with a three-point chain around my wrists, my belly, and down around my feet. The chains are all connected. They call it a three-point restraint, in case I decide to jog without permission. And of course, two guards go with me when I am out, one with a gun.

"On the way to and from the eye doctor's office I had to travel on an elevator. Loved that. On the way down there was this kid, about this high," he indicated with his hand the height of a small child. "He was with his mother in the elevator when I came down from the doctor's office. I was not supposed to start a conversation with anyone outside so I kept quiet. But it sure was good to see a child. It had been a lot of years for me since I saw a child outside."

"I never thought of that," I replied with momentary sadness for the things he had lost.

"Well, he kept looking up at me. He was about four, I think," he remembered. "I felt like he was going to hurt his neck looking all the way up to my full height."

He chuckled to himself as he thought about the child. That twinkle came to his eye.

"Well, the kid kept staring, and the mother was very polite. I think she was embarrassed or scared. She looked away, probably hoping the kid wouldn't say anything. I assumed she knew why I was dressed in orange and was in chains."

At this point I asked, "Are you embarrassed to wear the orange jumpsuit?"

"After being in prison, there is not much left that can embarrass you," he replied. The change of routine in going to the eye doctor outweighed the concern about clothing. "Next thing I knew, the kid was really straining his neck even harder to see all of me. He looked like he was going to say something. I knew I would answer if he spoke to me. He was so serious about something, and then he looked up and said, 'I know you.'"

"'Oh yeah' I said."

"'Yup. You're Santa Claus.'"

I laughed, knowing Charlie's white hair, mustache, and beard had created the image. His arms flew up behind his head as he joined me laughing, cracking up at his own story. Recalling the story again, he went into a full-scale belly laugh. I giggled even louder. Friends around the visit room joined with us, glad that in this austere place, there was some joy.

"That poor kid," I reflected. "Here he is just before Christmas. He's got the ultimate person here in the elevator with him. Santa isn't talking, but finally he gets bold and mentions the fact of who he is."

"Gotta wonder. I guess he figured Santa would be out and about this close to Christmas," Charlie finished.

With the innocence of a child, the boy had never questioned why Santa was riding on an elevator in an orange jumpsuit and saddled with three-point restraint chains. Not to mention that he seemed to be accompanied by armed guards.

People in prison often live with a great deal of depression. Yet in the midst of this darkness, Charlie's humor stood out as a bright light. His stories and witty remarks brought much-needed joy to many men behind the walls.

Another story Charlie loved to tell is about a new guard being trained in how to do strip searches. As Charlie finished dressing, the trainer commented to the new guard, "You better search the next guy real well."

Charlie, adding his two cents' worth of instruction, suggested, "Make sure you look everywhere on him, if you know what I mean." The poor fellow took Charlie seriously and quickly got down on his knees to look at the next man's butt. After all, we know from movies that this is what they do in prison searches. Right?

Later on, traveling to Warren with Kenny, a fellow from my church, I said, "Charlie told me a funny story." I told the gist of Charlie's strip search story but implied a more intimate body part in the retelling. Also, in my foggy version, Charlie was the victim of the new guard's search. I am a big-picture person and rarely can fathom the need for attention to detail. When Kenny and I got there, I shared with Charlie what I had told Kenny. Well, the *true* story, as Charlie told it, was even funnier because I had already told this erroneous and embarrassing account.

"You told him what?" he said, as his belly laugh expanded.

Part of the fun was Charlie correcting my version with great pizzazz.

Relishing every detail, he redid the tale for Kenny, this time in his best down-east accent. At the point of no return, when just looking at each other caused more laughter, the story matured into a side-splitting scene, the kind that makes the belly ache, with all three of us all pounding the table.

It never crossed our minds that the guards were not stopping us from creating a commotion. Charlie was glad he had met another member of our church, and we totally enjoyed our day. As for me, I loved my husband and was proud of him. Little did he know that something else was coming up that would be a story he would remember forever.

Chapter 21

A WONDERFUL SURPRISE

Not long after our marriage, Charlie called unexpectedly with a gush of excitement in his voice. "Honey, you will never guess who wrote me."

Now, I could not think of a single person who would make my husband so excited. "No, who?"

"My son," he said. It was his younger son, Burt. "He really wants to talk about his life. He also wants to meet you."

We had prayed so long for his kids, and this seemed almost too good to be true. "Of course I want to meet him too."

"I will send his letter home to you, and you can call or whatever so you can meet him."

"I will go see him as soon as possible," I assured him. "Get the letter to me."

We were filled with hope and praise that night. When the letter arrived, I waited until evening to call Burt. Because of my hearing loss, I do not like calling people I do not know, but I strained as hard as I could just to participate in this miracle. He was charming on the phone, and we made plans for me to take him to dinner near his home. It was another long drive, but wild horses could not keep me from this delightful task. I had slipped my camera onto the front seat. I knew that sending Charlie a photo of his son would bless my husband more than I could imagine.

"Hi, I am Kay, get in," I said to the fine-looking young man who stood waiting. Burt was a rugged woodsman, much like his father. I was soon to find out he was also very honest in conversation. His girlfriend was having a baby, another grandchild for Charlie to add to Burt's first two. He wanted to get his life together. Off we went to a local chicken joint and ordered our meals. Like his dad, Burt was easy to talk to, and before I knew it, we seemed like family. He even offered to help my son with a house remodeling job since he was a carpenter and jack of all trades. He had experience renovating and working for contractors.

At the end of the evening, we had planned still another meeting and dinner at my home. All of this was too exciting to even imagine. I couldn't wait to tell Charlie. But finally, the most joyous of all words came to my ears.

"I have not seen my father in ten years. I want to go with you to visits sometime soon."

"Oh my goodness," I exclaimed. "That would be the biggest blessing he has had in ten years."

"I know he would like it. And I want to surprise him."

"Uh-oh, he does not like surprises," I told him, thinking that Charlie must have changed during his time inside. Burt must have known him as a man who liked to be surprised. But I was wrong.

"I know," Burt said. "But I also know he will like this surprise."

Immediately I helped him schedule a visit with me. I did not want to miss this coming together of father and son. We worked out a date that was good for him and that fit into Charlie's work schedule at the wood shop. I reminded him that the prison had changed towns since the last time he'd seen his dad and gave some easy directions. One detail I neglected to tell him was that there was another prison facility on the same road before he would get to Charlie's prison.

The day of the surprise visit finally arrived. I was to meet Burt at the lobby of the prison, but visits were called and still he was not there. Going into the visit room without him was hard, but I was glad Charlie did not know because it would be another disappointment in his life.

What could I do? Enjoy my time with my husband. So we began our time together, catching up on things from our week apart. I was saying something very important, I thought, but suddenly I did not have Charlie's attention, not even a little. He first got a look of confusion on his face, and then he stood up and moved away from the table. This was not something he ever did. I turned, and Burt had arrived, a little mystified because he had first stopped at the other facility.

"Burt!" was all Charlie could say to his son. The look of elation on his face was priceless as he embraced his grown son. They shared something in that moment only a father and son can know. My heart leaped, and I gave Burt a hug too. At the end of the visit, Burt left a few minutes early, saying, "You two say good-bye alone."

Charlie hugged me good-bye, whispering, "That was the best surprise I have ever had." Burt was right. He did like some surprises.

Chapter 22

MY KID

H ow did you meet him? Why did you marry him? How will your marriage ever work if he has a life sentence?"

My son Aaron asked a barrage of questions when I went to visit him and his wife, Sally, after the birth of their new son. It was the first time I'd seen them since before my wedding, and it soon became obvious that my recent marriage was not making sense to Aaron.

I had come to help out with their new son, so Aaron asked me to help paint his bedroom. He actually did all the painting while we talked for what seemed like hours. He wanted more information about Charlie, and I was glad to give it. Aaron is a strong believer, and he's been a wonderful support to me through the years. Rude and rebellious are not in him; he is just inquisitive. He once sent me a book about the history of prisons, and later he would take me by the nearby Auburn Prison. His current questions and uneasiness seemed normal, considering his natural concern for his mother.

"You could fill out papers and come meet Charlie," I ventured. I thought he just wanted to know the circumstances of our relationship before planning to meet my husband.

"No," he replied. No explanation. He just did not want to meet Charlie.

I was determined to let my children and their spouses choose whether or not to meet my new husband. As Charlie said, "God gives choices, and we should too." Charlie's older son still would not meet me. It was too painful for him to even receive a letter from his father, let alone to meet me. Bringing families together is difficult, and our situation caused even more strain.

After we finished painting, we had dinner and I went to bed in the living room. Around two in the morning I woke up sorrowing over the predicament between Aaron and me. *Lord, keep me quiet so I will not disturb the family.*

I wanted my son to understand, and I wanted him to get to know Charlie. As I thought over the questions Aaron had posed the day before, the Lord comforted me with a Scripture encouraging me not to worry. I felt disappointed that Aaron and Charlie were not going to meet, but I finally let it go. Then I felt peace. God was God, and I slept.

We'd been invited to a church barbeque the next day. Sally encouraged us to go, but she decided to stay home with the boys. Off we went after making her promise to call our cell phones if she needed help.

The people at the cookout were from Aaron's new church. He only knew the host couple, and they were busy setting up and cooking. The husband seated us with two men. One was a relative of our host and not much of a talker. The other, an older man named Whitey, quickly engaged Aaron in conversation about the Lord. I enjoyed listening to them discuss their mutual love for Jesus and a variety of other topics.

At one point, Aaron asked Whitey, "So what do you think of the Auburn Prison?"

"Oh, I did some time there," came the surprising reply.

I sat up a little straighter. *Okay. You have my attention now, Lord.*

"Really?" my son's response seemed to encourage the man.

"Yes, and I did time at Attica and San Quentin too. I had a real life sentence," he said. That got my attention even more. A real life sentence is stronger than just a life sentence. It means the sentence *must* go to the end of life.

"Oh?" The huge question mark in Aaron's voice let our new friend know he had an audience glued to their seats, but still no understanding of why we were now listening so closely.

"Yup. Real life is a hard sentence. I knew I was going to be there for the rest of my natural life," he explained. "But then I met Jesus. I knew Jesus could do anything."

Lord, what is going on here? This is totally wild.

"Yes, I was doing time, and a local church ministry came in. They got me interested, and finally, I accepted the Lord. The volunteers came to the prison from the church that is hosting this picnic today. They were devoted to visiting people inside, and I knew they loved me."

My heart at this point was airborne. The Lord was doing something. I mean, what were the chances of this happening? It was so similar to Charlie's and my story. But managing to keep quiet, I forced myself to stay on the chair.

"Wow, you are out from a life sentence?" Aaron asked, shaking his head in disbelief. "How did it happen that you were released?" I was so grateful for his questions, because I wanted to know how Whitey had come to be released. Here was an amazing tale of God's mercy and the state's mercy, and I wanted to hear every detail. However, it did not seem wise for me to interject myself into the conversation.

Whitey continued. "Oh, well, I prayed for a chance to get out. But first things first. A woman soon came in with the ministry team, and we got talking. She was a light to the guys inside, along with the others from this church who kept coming."

"Oh?" Aaron questioned, keeping the conversation going and again shaking his head. It was all I could do not to stand and scream, "Whitey, tell the story faster!"

"Yup. She and I enjoyed each other's company when her team came in, so I invited her to come visit me. One thing led to another, and I asked her to marry me. So we got married inside the prison."

Aaron now looked more than amazed. To Whitey, we were just two people at the barbeque. He had no idea why I looked so eager for him to continue his story.

"Yes, it's been hard, but we worked out a lot of problems. We decided together to ask God if He would let me out."

Whitey's story was causing my heart to soar with new hope. Here was this former lifer sitting in front of me, obviously not in prison. It was like watching a fairy tale you want to end in a certain way, but not believing it will.

Noticing how riveted we were to his every word, Whitey explained more of this glorious event. "Yes, they had a program for release, and they told me what hoops to jump through. I had to move to another place and all. Moved to medium security, then to minimum. But finally they let me out on probation."

Will my heart explode before this is over? "Really?" Aaron blurted out with raw emotion in his voice. Now Whitey looked puzzled. People in prison learn to read others for survival. He seemed to be trying to figure out if we were glad he'd been released or whether we were people who felt no lifer should ever get out.

"Yes, it happened," Whitey said emphatically, maybe thinking Aaron did not believe him.

"Tell him, Mom! Tell him!" Aaron almost shouted. Shaking his head now, it was hard to miss the incredulity on Aaron's face.

"Tell me what?"

"Well, I am married to a man in Maine who is inside for a life sentence. I worked on Kairos retreats for people in prison. One thing led to another and I married Charlie inside, and we are praying for his release. Aaron spent the afternoon yesterday asking me all about it. Us meeting, our marriage, us praying for release. And now you tell us this incredible story!"

Whitey smiled in sudden understanding, knowing he was totally in God's plan for that day. No coincidence could be this exact. He assured me he would pray for Charlie. He gave me some pointers from his experience to share with my husband. I sat awestruck at the events of the afternoon.

I kept trembling and praising God quietly for this amazing adventure. When Charlie called that night, I had a wonderful yarn to tell him. And as Charlie and I were still doing time, we waited for release to come, working hard not to live in the "maybes." Sadly, we had no more contact with Whitey. But Charlie and I knew our meeting had been from the Lord.

Chapter 23
WHAT IS NORMAL LIFE?

W hat is normal life? My life moved to a certain rhythm before I met Charlie. Not a rhythm others might call normal, but it felt so to me. A nice mix of work and play, family and friends, missions and the mundane. At the center of it all was Jesus. My first encounter with God had reshaped my view of normal life. Now here I was following the Lord and married to Charlie. A new normal yet again.

"My life doesn't seem normal," I remarked to Charlie.

"What does that mean?"

I knew he wanted to know if marriage inside prison was upsetting me. "Well, I am just thinking. Other people think we do not have a normal marriage. But I am so content with the way it is going. What would we expect if we were out there and married? What would normal be?"

Is normal living in the manner in which you were raised? Following the norms of the culture around you? Abiding by some set of rules that someone has extracted from a holy book? For me the question was, "How does that express itself within our marriage now?" I had pondered this since we were married.

I met the Lord in 1977. Because of the overwhelming love that flowed to me on that day, I could no longer deny that God was real. A new normal. Now, married to Charlie, what would change? I would see what it meant to love my dear Charlie "for better or for worse."

Normal life for me became an adventure that first few years. Even though we lived far apart and had no conjugal rights, it was a time of discovery about each other and all the wonders of being married. I found a little plaque that read "Love knows no distance" and put that up by Charlie's picture at home as a reminder of our life together.

We learned early that a key to walking out marriage was to ask God for help when we got discouraged by what others tried to tell us was normal. We also wanted dearly to be together at home. Charlie still called his cell his house. But he now called Sanford his home.

Lord, how does this distance fit into Your plan for marriage? I asked. First of all, how were Charlie and I to achieve intimacy? I kept comparing our situation to those of others, not in a negative way, but to get an idea. In most marriages, people live together with privacy. We had to work for it. At one point a man who knew Charlie kept talking to him during our visit, interrupting us many times. All we wanted was to talk to each other. But this man kept interfering with us in some of our most personal moments whenever our visits coincided. Finally, when I got totally frustrated, I had to think about what was going on. After prayer, I realized that Steve was coming into our bedroom. Knowing he did not realize it, I quietly spoke to him, explaining, "This is our bedroom, and we don't want you in it. Before we embrace, we are outside our bedroom, and it is okay to talk to us. Once we sit, we have gone into our bedroom, and we spend those two precious hours with each other." He agreed, and it was not a problem again. More importantly, we began to catch a vision of how God would give us intimacy.

We had intimate conversations in the midst of a room filled with others. Charlie taught me that we just could not be concerned with saying things out loud to each other. This was the way it was in prison. This problem, thorny at first, was made more difficult because I could not hear Charlie if he whispered something personal.

So we learned to build intimacy. Often overseen at close range by guards, we continued. Captains marched through to take out a person who was suspected of passing contraband, and we continued. We were intimate among men who have done all manner of crimes against humanity, and we continued. Sitting at the table, it became the private place where no one else was invited as we two were becoming one.

Marrieds on the outside made time for each other. The prison scheduled our time with each other. Our conversations were within a regulated time: the time between "Visits!" and "Visits over!" This announcement that the visit had ended was much like an alarm clock for a couple not doing time in prison. At the call, our time of confidences ended. Comparing our circumstances to normal helped us to see that a lot was normal about what God had brought to us.

"Charlie, we found a way to invite people to our wedding without them able to come. You found a way to get out of the walls by carving animals from the Maine woods and streams. I am just looking for more ways to avoid restrictions that we put on ourselves because we see each other only inside the prison. Making myself conscious of it," I told him one day.

"Yeah, we have family in whenever we can get together. And I am meeting many of the River of Life people."

"You help me out a lot with expenses at home too, Charlie. We are involved in each other's lives," I mused to him. "And we file taxes together."

"Well, it doesn't really matter that much. Some things are just the way they are."

But I chose to try to identify what things I would like someday in our lives together. To myself, I listed more things that would be normal. My heart ached when I did this, so I did not do it much. I guess I was just expressing to God the desires of my heart. How could we ever have a cup of coffee together or share a meal? How could we ever receive communion together? How could we have a rip-roaring fight without upsetting the guards? Inevitably we would face having important fights while surrounded by others.

Eventually, all marriages get to the place of disagreement between the partners. With failed marriages behind us, we wanted to learn how to maneuver through highly emotional issues that came up. How on earth would that happen? Before we were married we'd had a few arguments, including the one very scary one just before our wedding. There had been resolution. So we could do it with forgiveness.

"Oh, we will discuss things when we disagree," my dearest assured me. I wondered if that was realistic since there would probably be bigger disagreements as time went on. If people do not argue, it is often because they are not being honest about what they are feeling. We were bent on being honest.

One fight we did have after our wedding was another alarming one. Charlie was upset about something I had asked him, and he refused to reply. I was determined to get my answer if it took the whole visit. I forged ahead. In different ways I kept asking, and he kept avoiding. We were both stubborn!

Finally he announced, "This is just like my first wife." He said it with emphasis, but not loudly enough to worry the guards. But it was quite clear to me how angry he was. Anger was frightening for me, but several times in my life with this man I had walked through some animosity successfully. I recognized now that I too had anger and that it was part of living. After the incident just before we were married, I had been made aware of just how angry I get at times. Not knowing what to do, and fearing rejection and Charlie's anger, it was me who was now not going to respond.

Having a disagreement in prison brings a unique set of obstacles. Violence is sometimes why people are in prison, so guards are trained to watch for any indication that it might be coming, such as loud outbursts. There have been couples in the past who have come to blows in the visit room. Added to that, there is the intensity of being watched every moment of every day in all that anyone does. There are no private places to let your feelings go. But this table was the place we had been given for this fight, so we plunged into uncharted territory for both of us. I am sure he was thinking of the other time when he had told me to get out. And I knew he did not want to do that again.

Charlie and I were two different kinds of fighters. When I got mad, I cried and pouted out loud. When he got mad, he exploded and yelled. You can do neither without raising the concern of the guards. Without emotional release, we just shut up. He turned his face away from me and looked out the window. His breathing was short and puffy. If he had been a cartoon, he would have had smoke coming out his ears.

I kept looking at him with tears rolling down my face, wondering facetiously when it was that we were going to talk everything over just as he had planned. If I had been a cartoon, I would have been the drama queen, with swollen red eyes and "When are you going to discuss this as *you* promised?" in my thought bubble. I was so angry I wanted to hold Charlie to this dumb plan of his. Both of us were going to have to learn to put our feelings into words without alarming the guards.

Time passed with us just sitting there, staring at the wood grain on the table, me with tears continuing, him puffing and fuming. With the Lord's gracious intervention, we both gradually began to talk real talk. We did not accuse or avoid, but our voices got as loud as possible without scaring the guards.

"I am not your first wife," I finally spoke up.

"Well, you have some funny ways of wanting to talk about something that is none of your business," he said, seeming to shut me out.

"It is my business if it is hurting me while we sit here with limited time to talk. A simple answer to my question would be good. It feels like you are closing me out because you are too tired to answer."

"I am not tired. I just decided that I don't have to tell you every little thing I do when you are nowhere around. And now it is getting us into a fight. In prison I have learned not to open my mouth until my insides calm down. I did that," he told me.

"Well, I cry when I am mad. I know I am bugging you, and I wanted an answer. I am sorry." I ventured, "You can keep it to yourself."

"Well, it does not really matter. I could just tell you. Sorry. I don't mean to cut you out of my life around here. I just get so upset sometimes that we can't be together all the time. I guess I am really just mad about that. Sorry."

Asking forgiveness of each other finally brought peace. To this day, I don't recall what it was I wanted him to tell me!

In the middle of strong feelings life does not always go as planned, but God's grace was there for us. Through it, the Lord drew us closer together.

Another time we had a fight on the phone. Charlie was having a really bad day. In fact, he had been having a hard week. Looking at the situation there in prison, it is no wonder he was ready to come down on everyone and everything, including me. He was running on about how he hated this and that. I ranted to him about people in my life too, so I could understand. But this time when he just needed me to listen, I felt I should lecture him about it. I should give him solutions.

"Charlie," I ventured, "you cannot go on with all this hate."

He blew up."You try living here before you say that!"

Charlie's explosion seemed to send me over the edge, but the truth was that I was sick of the system we were under. I wanted to hang up. I wanted to run away and stop this whole marriage. Now it seemed too much like my first marriage, and fear took over. Danger loomed in thinking he was like other men who had hurt me. Would I eventually get beaten up? Given his crime, I panicked. I hung up the phone with unresolved fear, wanting only to get away from him.

I spent that night in anguish, my stomach churning. Yet I knew that to admit my fear of him physically hurting me would wound him. Over the years various people had said things to him, cruel things, about his crime. But he could do nothing to change the past; he could only change himself. I knew he was a changed man from all our time together. But how could I be honest? He really needed to know I was scared. Either he would let me be real or we would not make it as a couple.

After almost thirty years of waiting for God to give me a husband, this was a desperately heartbreaking, alarming time for me. My thoughts went back to my brother's last advice to me, to be honest in my relationship with a man.

That Sunday, it was all I could do to get to the prison. I had prayed a lot and felt the Lord say that I should not bring it up, but wait until Charlie was ready. By the time I arrived, he was no longer angry. He was just as positive as could be. Finally, I dove partway into the pool of fear. And you cannot dive partway into a pool.

"Charlie, I did not mean to upset you the other night," I ventured. "It doesn't really matter if you want to vent with me."

"Truthfully, I was just waiting for you to come in here and complain. I was going to blast you more," he said with a tense smile. He was not sure how that would go over, admitting he was trying to set me up. "I know you're not a complainer."

"I decided not to harp on it, but to let you bring it up. But we need to talk. And you're right. I don't know what it is like for you here all the time."

"We'll do better next time. I hope."

We had both figured out where we could do better next time, but I had still not said the unthinkable. I wanted him to know my fear of his past so I could get beyond. I could not imagine how hard it was for him to know people would call his actions into question every time he got angry. And I did not want that hanging over us. Somehow it had to be said, and we had to let God fix us. But my fear of his anger would seem like I doubted the very change the Lord had done in him.

I knew my need for healing. I was torn, wanting to let Charlie know how his anger affected me but not wanting to wound him more. I well knew that in my first marriage the anger got worse when I shared the hard things. This was the most difficult place for both of us, but he did not even know.

Lord, I will talk and leave it in Your hands.

"Charlie, I don't want to hurt you. I know how people accuse you of being dangerous when you are angry. But I also have stuff I need to be honest about," I started.

"What's that, Dear?"

"Well, your anger and knowing your crime scares me at times. I don't think I would be normal if I did not feel that. I know you have changed. But I have to be honest. It ran through my mind when you yelled on the phone last week. Your crime, I mean."

Unthinkable. I had spoken the unthinkable.

I could see he was upset again. The longest silence we'd ever had came before he managed to speak.

"This hurts," he choked out. It made me ache to see his pain so clearly. But he was reaching deep to be honest. More time passed as we collected our thoughts.

He spoke first. "Honey, I know when I have scared you. I am sorry. It's okay to talk and tell me. You know all about me, and we will work it out," he said. We were talking, not avoiding our problem. I wanted to dance. And I also wanted to soothe his heart.

I reached across the table and took his hand. A gentle touch conveying more than my words could express. "Charlie, I love you."

He squeezed my hand and said, "I love you too."

Charlie's willingness to be there in every way for me allowed me to give myself totally to him. I have met no other man as open and honest and willing to face honestly a difficult past. Songs to God came naturally all the way home that day. Marriage was indeed the hardest work we would ever do, but it was also the most rewarding.

Here is part of a prayer I sent Charlie the next day:

Father God, today I just want to come to You in thanksgiving for the deepening of our relationship that has taken place. We have both walked into some painful areas of our lives. We are talking about things I never thought I could share. I think Charlie had no idea he could talk like this either. But we are in a new relationship today. We have found another place in our love for each other. We have found a higher level of friendship. We trust. Father, it is Your love, trust, friendship. Father, what a miracle that two messed-up human beings could be so in love, so in trust, and so in friendship. What a rare and precious jewel You have given us.

Chapter 24

DREAMS OF HOME

I n the spring of 2005, at the same time Charlie and I were planning our upcoming marriage, he applied for clemency. Clemency was one of two legal possibilities in Maine at the time for someone who had a life sentence. It meant mercy could be granted after a good number of years because the person had changed and was no longer a danger to society. He or she was now able to function as a law-abiding citizen. Clemency is a second chance for those who are not habitual criminals. The other possibility was home confinement.

No one of us should be remembered for a lifetime because of our worst deed unless we have not changed. In prayer, I tried to convince God of the need for Him to get Charlie clemency.

Maine removed parole from the books in 1976. At the time of sentencing a judge cannot know if a person will change, but with parole, if a person *does* change inside, at the time for review he can earn early release. For example, a sentence might be life with the possibility of parole after twenty-five years. The remaining sentence can be served outside, thus practicing freedom while still under the Department of Corrections. Parole would still last until the end of the sentence, and the person would go back to serve the rest of his sentence if he was not law-abiding during that time. In other words, parole is used only where one demonstrates good behavior over many years of his sentence. The Department of Corrections is supposed to correct people, so logically parole would motivate people to participate in their correction. Parole says we believe in second chances.

Probation is tacked on to the end of a sentence and is very difficult to navigate. Those with probation don't get out early but rather have one sentence inside and then one outside, with added difficult restrictions such as never being in a house with any alcohol. It is difficult to know if someone has alcohol in their home!

There is a scientific way to show change. There are checklists to determine if a person who committed a nonviolent or violent crime is now a low-risk person. When a person has demonstrated a change, a good parole board will judge whether or not he or she is safe to release with a set of measurable standards. The person released must stay on the right side of the law, proving the change.

Pardon is another option, but the granting of pardon means that the governor (or the state) recognizes a person is not guilty of the crime. Since Charlie honestly admitted that he was guilty of his crime, pardon was not an option for us. Clemency for those who have committed a crime is mercy. You are granted what the judge originally did not think you deserved. But in the real world, releasing the guilty becomes political, and it has been that way since Pilate released Barabbas.

With this in mind, knowing that Maine has no parole, we submitted all the letters and the application for clemency, along with all the required court records. It was a time of prayer and hope, waiting and anguish, knowing an answer would come. We were both novices at this. Charlie had never bothered to try before because he had no supportive family; he had expected to live out his years inside the walls. Now his hopes were up, along with mine. We did know that we would either rejoice with homecoming or face an unthinkable. Overcoming the inevitable disappointment of not being granted clemency would perhaps be the end of this journey.

The Clemency Board met four times a year and decided the clemency bids that were sent to them. Our time was fast approaching. Somehow we began to attend to other things in our lives. Charlie was back to work in the wood shop, and I continued to build the neighborhood friendships back home.

But we dreamed. When Charlie came home we hoped he could talk to the kids around us about staying out of trouble with the law. He would have to report to a probation officer, but maybe we could work it out that he would work with kids. He desperately wanted to share his experience with the kids around home so they would not get life in

Maine like he had. He felt that it was gradual, the road from simple untamed anger to doing something under the influence that carries a life sentence. If they knew where the road of anger had taken him, he could pay society back in some measure for what he had done. He would never go back to prison if he got a second chance. He was stubborn in that way.

Maybe our biggest dream was to sit at the kitchen table and have a cup of coffee together. Would the Lord grant us that?

Then came the visit when he told me. "Honey, we have some bad news. I got the answer from the Clemency Board, and they will not grant me a meeting with the governor."

I processed that as well as I could. "Okay, we go forward from here. We both know God is in control, no matter what the governor says," I replied.

A heavy sinking feeling only begins to describe how we felt as we tried to take in the information together at the table. The death of our dreams. Charlie was experiencing it with me and had tried not to think about it until I was with him. We held hands, and I cried silent tears as I looked into his watery eyes. My special man was devastated to have to tell me this. I knew he would prefer to just keep it to himself, but we were married.

"Charlie, I know it is hard for you mainly because of me. I know that. My heart aches for you." He just nodded.

Our dream was dashed to pieces right there in front of guards and other visitors. Although the long wait for an answer to Charlie's clemency petition was finally over, this meant we must face the possibility that he might only be released when he died.

It was a toss-up as to who was more upset that day when we received the first rejection. I was upset because of my innocence of the ways of the justice system at that point. Charlie always got upset when I did. One month and twenty-four days after the wedding, Charlie had read,

"The Board did not find your petition to demonstrate exceptional circumstances to warrant a hearing at this time. Although there is no single definition or standard for 'exceptional circumstances,' at a minimum, you must demonstrate a compelling substantial and sustained effort to lead a positive and productive life over an extended period of time…"

Charlie had demonstrated such an effort over and over to me and to others. In my first meeting with the assistant commissioner, she had said he was certainly the most changed man she had ever met in the system. Guards had also alluded to this as I got to know them along the way. Because of Charlie, many of my friends outside had started to see prisoners as people who can change rather than people who should be locked up for life. He was not the sociopathic person many saw on TV. They wanted him home. I certainly knew in my whole being that he had not meant to kill the woman he killed. My heart fairly raged inside me as I thought about the menacing reality of his being turned down.

That night, I prayed for acceptance. By morning the Lord led me to Psalm 77:6:

I call to remembrance my *song in the night:* I commune with mine own heart: and my spirit made diligent search. (emphasis added.)

Somehow our devastation would be turned into a love song in the night. A love song behind the walls of prison. It would be a constant prayer to the God who beheld us.

Only later would we learn exactly just how political this clemency decision was. Only later would we realize there is no mercy in a system that holds elderly people inside, no matter how sick or disabled or corrected they are. Only later would I be told that only when death is imminent would the system grant mercy. And even then . . .

It was a mammoth struggle to hold on to God. We began the enormous task of receiving what He wanted.

"God could release me tomorrow if He wanted."

"God is in absolute control. He can do anything," I replied. I knew that deep in my heart. But for today, this was how it would be. This was real. The walls were solid, and we still lived two-and-a-half hours apart.

Inadequate as it is to try to write about such a juncture, after a lot of discussion and tears, a measured acceptance and peace came to both of us. Somehow we still had faith. Now we both knew that God would receive *all* the glory if Charlie came home to me here on this earth. And if Charlie did not come home, God would use that somehow for good.

After the 2005 clemency request was turned down, Charlie and I talked it over at visits for several weeks. Sorting it all out was good for us. We accepted what seemed inevitable. He and I would not be together at home for now. We would take on living one day at a time again, knowing God had a good plan for us. What would it be?

By the fall of 2006 we were going along building our marriage and also having friends from church meet him. He was now a member of River of Life.

During one visit he said to me, "A cop came and told me something good was going to happen for the long-timers this fall."

"Well, what does that mean?" I asked.

"I don't know, Dear. I asked him, and all he said was, 'I did not say that.'" One more emotional roller coaster that would probably result in nothing, but we wondered.

During that time, Charlie was also trying to explain the difference between parole and probation to me.

"The old parole system was better than probation," said Charlie.

"Why?" I questioned.

"Probation is to make sure you are doing well outside. It's supposed to help. The problem is," he continued, "the time is added to a sentence. If you have thirty-five years, there can be ten more added if you do not exactly follow all the conditions of probation. So it is a sentence on top of a sentence. The second sentence is for an infraction of a condition of probation, not necessarily for breaking a law."

"How do they decide the length of the probation?"

"Well, the judge determines that at sentencing. At best it is a guess tacked on to a guess for the time it will take for a person to be corrected. You may have to stay away from your old neighborhood. You cannot be around alcohol. If you are at a neighbor's house and someone sees beer there, you can be reported and go back to serve the second sentence," Charlie told me. Even a disgruntled neighbor could report and send someone back.

I was starting to understand. But I had a lot more to learn.

"So how is parole different?" I continued.

"You get your time, and if you are doing well, are changed, and have no write-ups, you get heard by the parole board early. They can let you go early. Then the only reason you would come back is if you commit a new crime. And you still have to finish your time. Still under the Department of Corrections until your sentence is up. Saves the state a good lot of money."

Parole is a cleaner release, only asking you to show you are reformed. "This does seem to be more like it would motivate someone. Give hope," I remarked. "Coming out is hard enough without having added restrictions. Coming out on parole, all you have to remember is don't commit a crime. And stay in touch with the parole officer."

"Yeah," Charlie said. "There have been lifers who got out on parole after twenty-five years and succeeded better than some guys with a shorter sentence. The DOC used to believe a man could make a terrible mistake and could change. But even so, I would take probation. Actually, now I would take *anything* if they'd give me a second chance."

Charlie was arrested in the late 1970s at a point where the politicians were saying, "Lock 'em up and throw away the key." Thankfully, intelligent judges have seen that having longer and harsher sentences does not correct people, so sentences for similar crimes now are generally shorter. People can change.

During another visit, Charlie almost whispered, "An officer came and told me I had to have my picture taken this week."

"Why?" I asked.

"Who knows? Maybe to decorate my folder," he laughed. "They do it every ten years or so to make sure our file picture looks like us as we get older."

"So?" I said.

"So I don't know why they wanted to do it. I asked around and no one else is having it done. It is strange because they just took my picture when we moved to Warren five years ago."

We wondered more.

At visits again, where we did most of our talking, Charlie told me about still another incident.

"I get reclassified every year or so. And they just sent my papers. They had to decide about a bunch of things, like do I stay in close security or do they send me to medium? Everyone has to do it around once a year."

"What does that mean, Charlie? What do you do?"

"I fill out more papers. They ask me stuff. Then they fill out papers on me too, and it all goes in to classification. They classify me and send back the new classification. Funny thing is every year for the twenty-eight years I have been here, it has come back, 'Murder One, Life,' and this time it said 'Murder One, Probation?'"

"What does the question mark mean?"

"If I didn't know better, I'd think they were considering me for probation. But I have nothing to go on—just the question mark."

"Do you have the paper?" I was eager to see the word "probation" and the mysterious question mark.

"No. I just had to sign it and give it back. I didn't get a copy," he replied.

We both wondered what to make of this striking development.

Having received this puzzling piece of information, our minds raced to maybes again. Maybe his picture would have to be on documents for release. Maybe some higher-up had had mercy. Maybe there would be a new program in the fall for release of long-timers, like the Life Line they have in Canada. Or like Whitey had in New York. Considering all the possibilities left our nerves raw, but it was dreadfully hard not to look at all this.

Probation question mark became a constant echo in my head as I struggled to let go and turn to God. Time wore on, and the questions continued.

A couple of months later, Charlie came to visits with this story:

"My social worker gave me some more paperwork the other day. And *another* form for classification. They never classify you twice in one year," Charlie said. I could feel the restraint in his voice as he told me this new mystery. He added, "Besides, I never saw this form before. It was different from the other reclassification forms."

Again, Charlie had asked what this was for, and the social worker said, "I am not allowed to talk about it."

"What was the form all about?" I probed for any hint of why this was happening.

"I don't know, but the social worker asked, 'If you were to get out, where would you go? Do you have a place you could go if you could get out?'"

"Probably to my wife's place."

"Oh, are you married?" The social worker seemed surprised.

"You signed the permission."

"Oh, I remember something like that. Tell me her name and address and phone number." Now my information was on a form that had to do with classification as a possible place to go if Charlie got out. Strange.

Maybe they will decide to put me in close security with Charlie, I thought with a silly smile. "How come they want my address now? And my phone number?" I had always worried that somehow my lack of hearing would cause us to lose some chance we would get.

Charlie explained, "Well, sometimes they call a wife before a guy even knows he is getting out. I know that's happened before. They tell the inmate on the morning he is leaving so problems don't come up from jealousy. And the family can come and pick up the person if he has family."

My wondering became constant at this point.

We had been turned down for clemency because supposedly Charlie had not shown a sustained effort to change. He had changed. The staff knew that. They were hinting that probation was in the air. But we'd had so many disappointments that we could not get our hopes up, especially me. I knew one of Charlie's deepest concerns was that I was so new at this that I would be hurt again and again. His dilemma was that he wanted to share what was going on at these mysterious meetings inside when I was not there with him without unduly setting me up to be hurt.

Jacob wrestled all night. We wrestled a lot with these tiny indications that something was afoot behind the scenes, and we knew God was allowing all of this to come to our attention. To *not think* about it was the struggle of a lifetime for me at that point. But things could get worse.

Chapter 25
THE PRISON INFIRMARY

Honey, I cannot make it to the afternoon visit. I am really sick today. I can't face the strip search again today after the effort it takes just to get dressed in the morning." On that day in 2008, we were talking toward the end of our morning visit at the prison. Charlie was not able to do what was required of him to visit; he had been out of it during our whole time together, kind of sleepy and not hearing what I was saying. The pain in his leg was fierce.

It wasn't the first time. His diabetes was starting to interfere seriously with us seeing each other. Up until this time, we had been doing regular visits—two in one day each week and an occasional extra one per month that he got because he was in close security. Now I feared we would lose the visits we were permitted because he was too sick to do a strip search.

With tears in my eyes, I said, "Okay. I will see you next week." For the first time I walked out of a visit knowing he was too sick to come to me again. Charlie knew that I had traveled a long way. One of the reasons we had two visits on the same day was it was easier travel-wise for me to do both while I was there.

Just outside the lobby door as I was leaving, a kind friend stopped me. "Are you coming to the visit this afternoon?"

I told her what had happened and began to cry. She comforted me with a hug. Only someone who knew how important the restricted time for a visit was to someone in prison could hug and give wordless comfort like that.

On the drive home, my cell phone rang. I can still remember where I was on the road because this was another pivotal point for us. I recognized Tiny's voice, but it wasn't his usual friendly tone. "Hi, Kay, Charlie gave me your number so I could call in an emergency. He was admitted to the prison infirmary today. He never came back from visits." My heart sank, not knowing what to do. Should I drive back or go home? They would probably not let me see him, and I was right outside Sanford when Tiny got through. What could I do to help him? Nothing was ever normal, try as we might. *What now, Lord?*

I could once again hear Charlie saying, "Sweetheart, there is absolutely nothing you can do about it. Only God can." His strength of character had been forged in the pits of this hell called prison, and it spoke to me now.

Being sick didn't just affect our visits. Charlie had worked all his life, including after he went to prison. Going to work was extremely important to him for his dignity, and he couldn't work if he was in the infirmary. They also regularly gave away jobs if someone could not get to work.

Charlie hated being confined in the infirmary. Consequently, even if he wasn't feeling well, he got out of the infirmary as quickly as they would let him. Thus began the years of illness that entailed visits and no visits. Often I would drive the one-hundred-plus miles and go inside to sign the visit book with no reason to suspect I could not have a visit. I would wait fifteen minutes, and then the desk officer would tell me Charlie had refused the visit. It got so I dreaded the phone ringing in the lobby after I arrived because it would be someone calling to say Charlie could not come.

Finally, a kind sergeant—after hearing how far I drove—said to call ahead and ask if Charlie would have a visit that day. He said the desk could call down and find out for me, thus saving me some time in driving. But by the time he would know if he was well enough for the visit, I was often already almost up there. I would have already gone 95 of the 110 miles. Still, often I called so I would not have to face the lobby. In later years, Charlie was able to call me to tell me that he wouldn't be able to come.

Charlie was allowed out of the infirmary to come see me, but he could not go back to his cell when having an intravenous antibiotic for infection in his leg. The saline lock for the IV needles was allowed in the visit room, but he still had to return to the infirmary for the antibiotic. Sometimes he came to see me in a wheelchair, but he would abandon it outside the room and walk through the strip search and then to me at our table. When he walked, the pain on his face was obvious as he favored the leg with every step he took. Guards in the visit room began placing us at a table by the door where the inmates entered so he would not have to walk as far. I was grateful for this effort, but the other inmates coming in and out increased the noise level, which exacerbated my hearing impairment. Thankfully I could not see the future, where one merciless guard would place us a long way across the room, having Charlie walk on his bad leg.

More than once Charlie told me, "Honey, there are days when I am just too tired to face the strip room. It is too much work." When that happened, I would be told again, "Charlie has refused the visit." That is prisonese, meaning he could not come to the visit. When I first starting having my visits refused, I would go home feeling rejected. Much later, I realized it was the capriciousness of prison rules that kept us apart. Charlie would have loved to visit if they could have made an exception because he was so sick and let him skip the strip search.

A few times I asked why Charlie could not visit, and they told me they were not allowed to tell me that due to privacy laws. As a teacher I understand privacy laws, but I never withheld important health information from the family. I prayed that I would not harden my heart against the guards. They were just carrying out orders from above.

Sometimes Charlie could not visit because a doctor had ordered some test, like an EKG or a visit to an outside doctor. He was trying his best to get well, and I had to accept that this wasn't about me. Gradually most officers changed to telling me Charlie could not come because he was not feeling well.

Each day of visits in 2008, I entered the prison lobby with dread, fearing he would not be able to see me. One day I came and signed in. So far, so good. I sat to wait the half-hour before all the visitors would be sent through the metal detection machines in preparation for going down the hall to see our loved ones. I treasured hearing the word "Visits." But it was early yet. They have you sit a half-hour as they fetch the men up to the visit room from their pods when they know a visitor has come for sure. Any movement in a prison is complicated.

A sergeant I knew walked over to me and said, "Come on, Kay."

I tentatively replied, "You didn't call visits."

"I know. Come with me."

I didn't know how to react. *Please God. He did not call visits. He is only calling me to come. Oh, no, Lord. They are taking me out back to a quiet room to tell me Charlie has died. God, help…*

I followed the man and tried to keep composed, but my tears just would not stop.

"He's okay, Kay," the officer assured me.

My mind was bordering on panic, and I thought, *This is not the way to the visit room.* I was led right past the visit room sally port and through another one of those vast, impenetrable security doors.

God, I cannot do this without You. Please be with me. Help me not to be paralyzed with fear.

We walked around a corner and turned left into a new area, through another door toward our final destination. A little way inside I realized that the place looked vaguely familiar to me. I was in a hospital and could see a nurse's station.

Oh no, I must be going to the morgue. It has to be right behind the infirmary. Lord. Help me.

Then the officer said, "He's down there," pointing. Would he be sending me into a morgue all alone?

Now I took careful, measured steps. I saw a small room a few yards down the hallway. There was Charlie, sitting in a huge hospital lounge chair. Relief flooded over me as I returned his welcome smile.

He called out, "It is okay. You can come in here."

Gathering my wits, I forced my rubbery knees to move forward so I could kiss Charlie. It was a little strange to bend over him, having always stood to greet each other. It got even stranger when I realized I was in a cell with him.

Until this time, I had not realized how much the diabetes was sapping Charlie's health. He could not get up, and he looked very pale. I suddenly noticed the weight he had lost in his hands. They looked like an old man's hands. He desperately needed proper food to help turn around the illness, but the prison made no provision for such needs.

Once in Charlie's arms for a moment, my familiar place, I looked around the cell. It occurred to me that this room must look a lot like his "house."

"Is this cot like the one you have at your house?" I asked.

"Yup. About the same."

Except for a TV at the foot of the bed, the room looked cold and sterile. No pictures on the wall or anything personal.

"See the sink-toilet unit?" he asked. "It is all one piece. Nothing to make weapons with."

Much like I sometimes gave a tour of the house in Sanford, Charlie was giving me a tour of his hospital cell. We both knew it was as close as I would ever get to seeing his house.

"Can they see you while you are using the toilet?" My modesty was showing.

"Yes, but they don't often care. They know I'm not about to cause trouble."

The lounge chair took up most of the aisle between the bed on one side and the sink unit on the other. Someone had brought an extra chair for me to sit in while visiting. It was cramped.

At first I was self-conscious. I had never seen Charlie in anything except his prison blues. The sweats he was wearing looked like pajamas, and on the bed were a pair of his undershorts, which of course I had never seen. Somehow, I had pictured that seeing his underwear for the first time would be in a private place, not in a prison cell. Normally a wife might make a funny comment on this, but I figured eyes were on us. So I kept quiet. Talk about a shy bride—seeing my husband in anything other than his prison blues for the first time brought on embarrassment, and me old enough to be on Medicare!

Charlie showed me his foot and the bandages around his toes. He had an infection in his toes, so I saw his bare foot for the first time. Was I blushing over seeing his toes? I had left home at the same time as always that day and signed in as usual, and now here I was in his bedroom. *Was this really happening? And why?* I told myself that we were married and it was okay, but it felt slightly indiscreet. Especially knowing we were on camera. Once again, we were having an intimate moment in public, under the watchful eye of the Department of Corrections. Later we would jokingly refer to this as another honeymoon.

Charlie sensed I felt as awkward as he did about me being in his bedroom. Right next to his bed. Somehow it was as strange for him as it was for me. After all, he had not had a wife in his cell ever. And he'd had no idea the authorities would let me come down there for the visit until it happened.

"Charlie and I spent time together in his bedroom last visit," I told friends with a smile.

In our next regular visit in the visit room, Charlie told me with a twinkle in his eye, "No one was watching us that day except God." We laughed. We both knew that someone would have shown up if we'd tried anything beyond a brief kiss and hug.

I did know one thing for sure after that day. I was seriously going to pray that I would be with Charlie when he died—at home or at the prison or wherever. I could not handle knowing he had died alone. God willing.

My struggles were far from over. After that new experience of brief visual intimacy with Charlie and the reality of diabetes, I was soon to fall into another trap that would hurt my husband.

Chapter 26

IN CHAINS AND ORANGE

D oing time as a prison wife can be painful. All the mysterious things that happened to make us wonder if he was going to come home had not brought any fruit. The loneliness, the long drives, the struggles with prison rules, the worries about Charlie's health, the difficulty of communication, and the disappointments of being turned down for clemency kept grinding away at my spirit.

We'd been married over five years now, and I came to the awful conclusion that our romance was gone. No more flowers. No more pictures. No more spark in our relationship. Charlie had fallen asleep for the last half-hour of our Sunday visit. I couldn't blame him. His health had continued to worsen after our meeting at the infirmary.

I cried most of the way home. By the time I arrived, my list of complaints against God and Charlie was growing by the minute. My heart longed for all the wonderful things an ideal marriage contained, and it twisted over the disappointments in ours. Yes, I had accepted long ago that ours would not be a normal marriage, but I had never imagined it would be this hard. I wanted God to change things, to give me my way.

I decided it was time to convey my hurt to Charlie. To try to bring back some romance, by forcing the issue if need be. I fired off a letter expressing my disappointment and anger, and I mailed it on Monday morning. By Tuesday, I suspected I had made a mess of everything and panicked. My mood swung back and forth like a pendulum on a clock. Being apart from each other most of the time, I had thought Charlie would never see these, my mood swings, but they were on full display now. *Somehow God always brings into the light what is hidden in darkness.* One moment I wanted to apologize for everything. The next minute I was sure our marriage was doomed.

Finally, I wrote another letter apologizing for all I had said in the first one. I desperately wanted our marriage to continue, and I was exploding with feelings of anger and bewilderment, due to my own brokenness but also because a prison marriage is difficult. I also related to Charlie that I did not know what was happening to me but that I'd felt dead inside after I left the last visit.

Charlie called that week, sounding worse than I had ever heard him. He had just received the letter full of my roller-coaster emotions, and I could feel the pain in his voice.

"You have hurt me, and I don't understand," he said with such brokenness that I cringed. "Maybe we *should* end the marriage."

"Charlie, I wrote a letter in frustration and anger, more at the way things are than at you. I don't know why I aim it at you. I just do. Sweetheart, please forgive me?" I asked. "I sent another letter asking your forgiveness. It will be there probably tomorrow." Having to communicate by letter was another frustration because it was mixing up the issues.

He said he forgave me and then went on. "Honey, I just wrote you an awful letter this morning and mailed it. I told you not to visit again." He was being as transparent as I was, but it was very thorny for us to hear each other. I knew I wanted transparency, and I was finding out just how hard it is to walk that out.

"Will you forgive me? Pay no attention to the letter," he asked.

When his letter came, I was prepared. In it, he mentioned that we ought to think about whether our marriage was ever going to work. Thankfully, I got another letter on Saturday saying he wanted me to come up Sunday, as he had told me on the phone. Even the almost broken muffler on my car did not deter me from setting out for Warren. I left at the usual 5:15 a.m. the next morning, buying coffee before the turn onto the highway. I could not imagine what we would talk about all day. I was afraid of my own raw emotions. They were all over the place. I turned on my MP3 player and tried to worship God, but I was not honoring Him in my heart and I knew it. I languished in my own misery for most of the drive.

If Charlie was sick and unable to visit, he would call me so I would not drive the whole way unnecessarily. He had not called, so I felt assured the visit was on. As I was pulling into the prison parking lot, the cell phone rang. I scrambled to grab the phone out of my bag but missed the call. It was from a friend waiting inside to visit her fiancé. I called her right back.

"The guard said Charlie was not coming to visits. He was not feeling well."

"Thanks," I replied. "I'll leave without coming in." I was grateful. I left the property, never even turning off the engine of the car.

Then my mind sidetracked again, thinking Charlie must be mad at me. In my head I could hear "Get the hell out," as he had said before we were married. He was rejecting me, and my thoughts were so real that my heart was in pain again.

Oh Lord, heal me of this plague of rejection that hovers over me.

This was my Charlie, my love gift from God. The anguish and shock of another canceled visit were overwhelming. I relived the sorrow and hurt of all the years without a loving mate in one final moment, one final blast, as I pulled out of the driveway of Maine State Prison onto the road home. I screamed out my hurt just to relieve the pressure in my gut. No tears. Just deep screaming, dry screaming. Gradually, as with all deaths, I had seen the reality of our marriage.

Arriving home, I could not face the empty house. I was making renovations, making a nest for Charlie and me. But now I needed to be with someone, so off I went to my friend Pat's, almost around the corner. We went out to have coffee.

After my brief retelling of the morning events, she said gently, "The mind is not always right. Maybe he was really sick."

"How come he is not calling?" I demanded.

"Maybe he was sleeping or could not get to the phone," she reasoned. That was very logical. My thinking could be off. How much longer would it take me to be healed of rejection? She prayed, and I calmed down a bit.

At noon the phone rang, and it was Charlie's familiar phone exchange on my caller ID and a voice saying, "You have a call from an inmate at Maine State Prison." Hope came.

I pressed the code to receive the call, and we began.

"Hi, Charlie. I missed you. Sorry you were sick," I said as I thought of how scared I had been that he had no illness but just did not want to see me.

"I was so sick. I had pain in the night, my legs again. I knew I could not go through the strip search. I'm sorry."

Countless other men in my life had wanted to end things when the going got tough for them. Any excuse was fine. Husbands are to love their wives as Christ loves the church, laying down their lives for her as the Bible says. Charlie was laying down his life for me, daring to phone this unpredictable woman he had married. But I still needed to capture something more. What was still not right with me?

Lord, will You give me revelation so I can be tight with Charlie again, with no nagging doubts?

It took a few days, and I was still riding small waves of fear and doubt, but the Lord gently showed me the problem. I found myself at a meeting at church, crying for no apparent reason. At these meetings we interceded for the church as well as our own personal needs. We often asked the Lord what He wanted to say to us. Some verses in Psalm 102 caught my attention. I felt the Lord was trying to show me something, but nothing specific stood out. As we prayed, I read the verses again and again. Obviously, it had a line about prisoners, but I still did not understand. It felt like pushing to give birth early. No matter how hard I pushed, understanding was not there. I would have to wait. The prayer at church ended without me ever even saying anything about the psalm.

In the midst of all this, we had decided we would apply for clemency again. My one request was that I could come in to meet with the lawyer. Charlie welcomed the idea of having both of us go over the details of the application. I left the visit where we planned this new clemency bid and asked a sergeant if I could have permission to come in when Charlie met with his lawyer. He said that was beyond his authority, but he gave me information on who to contact and what the protocol might be. I was so thankful for his help and scribbled down the phone number of the woman I was to call.

The next day I followed the sergeant's instructions. The contact person told me that I would have to submit a written request and state that I wanted a onetime meeting with Charlie and the lawyer. She told me how to address it and said to call if I needed further help. I got off the phone and typed the letter. It was at least a good distraction, if not a cause for hope.

I turned on my phone to find a voice mail. It was from the office I had called on Monday: they had approved a onetime legal meeting, which did not count as a personal visit, with Charlie, the lawyer, and me. We could talk about clemency. Charlie was going downhill with diabetes, so he had a compelling reason to be home to get the right food, rest, and care.

Lord, this is all connected somehow.

After listening to my voice mail, I heard the phone ring, and this time it was Charlie.

"Hey, I got a call from the security department, and the secretary said it was okay for us to both meet with the lawyer," I told him.

"Great," he said. "I never did hear of such a thing. Never heard that someone could have their wife with them at a legal visit. Praise God."

Receiving permission to have family there when Charlie would meet with his lawyer made us happy. It was a normal family thing to do, and we would be doing it. Maybe we would get clemency, although our governor had never granted one clemency in two terms. (He finally did grant one woman a clemency who apparently only had a few months left to serve.) We did meet, but decided with the lawyer that it would be better not to apply for clemency at that point.

The next morning, I got up to pray and seek the Lord, and of course I looked at Psalm 102 again. It read:

For He hath looked down from the height of his sanctuary; from heaven did the LORD behold the earth; to hear the groaning of the prisoner; to loose those that are appointed to death. (Psalm 102:19–20)

One version of the Bible says the Lord gazed on the earth. Gazed. That means to look for a long time, not just a glance. So the Lord gazed from His place on high, looking intently at Charlie as he groaned. The Lord stopped and took time to lovingly look on Charlie in his pain.

Here I was, foolish and demanding romance, busy in my own self-pity, and the Lord was listening to Charlie's groans. Yet I could not take the time to hear Charlie's pain. And I had in effect told him that I was tired of his groans. Charlie had been sharing the extreme difficulties of his life there in prison, but I would not listen. If my Lord listened to my husband's groans, what made me think I should not? How could I live in my childish world and not listen to his daily difficulties and the repetitive dark happenings that go on in prison? I could scarcely contain my shame.

Charlie wore chains and orange when he was traveling outside. I, who live outside, was being released from my own chains and orange, my own prison of not caring. I could finally be compassionate again toward my husband, to the groans of this wonderful man who hurt so much of the time.

It was a breakthrough in itself. But more than that, God was preparing me for more adversity.

A wise friend once said to me that God is not a strict schoolteacher, testing us on our behavior. God is kind and good in all His dealings with us. I needed to recall this truth; it seemed God was building my faith through affliction.

Did I have what it took to stand in difficulty? Did I have the total trust I need to face things in our life together? Was I ready to follow Him no matter what it took? Jesus went to the cross for me. He gave His life. My mind said I was willing, but my heart was often anxious. It is okay to not be rich. It is okay to have an old car. It is okay to shop at Goodwill. In fact, I enjoy "treasure hunting" at thrift stores. But was it okay to *not* to have Charlie come home? The question seemed to overshadow every day of my life with Charlie.

Charlie was still inside. Where was the miraculous release? I surmised the Lord must want it this way; otherwise the release would have come. No doubt there. Somehow this was all part of a bigger plan in which the Lord would glorify Himself. But what was that plan?

I began the long, lonely process of renewing my mind with the washing of the Word. Life became richer as we faced the good and bad together. I knew God would take all that appeared to be hardship and use it to bring us to something even higher. He would use all the bits of shock and make a rich tapestry for us, beyond what we could think or imagine. Moving all that from my head to my heart was a slow, discouraging process. I enjoyed doing practical things to prepare for Charlie's release. I had a shower installed along with the tub, and I purchased a big bed, both physical reminders of the hope still unfulfilled, often making my heart sick. Could the dreams finally not matter?

Though we had applied for clemency again, that hope was always slim and could not be allowed to rule my thoughts. As time wore on, this dreaming had to be rooted out of my thinking. Daily I would trudge many times to the cross, laying another thought or dream at the feet of Jesus. Violent emotional assault on my mind, body, and spirit was constant and often squeezed the breath out of me. I would be having a pleasant day, and suddenly the thought would strike: *You never will have Charlie home, and your marriage is a failure* again. How could I move out of this? Fill my time with television? I did not want that. Not as a lifestyle. Not go see Charlie? That was unthinkable. I loved being with him even though we seemed to have less and less time. It was very difficult to shut down that normal part of us that wanted to be together. Although I knew we were together in our hearts, the reality of not living together was sometimes harder than I could bear.

Why, Lord? I cried too often at night. That was dangerous thinking, because it was not trusting what Jesus was doing. For Charlie, there was little hope of an end to his sentence. That was the bare reality of my life. To learn to live with this daily, I had to let go again and again. Just when I felt I was doing well, something else would happen to remind me that I had to give up our future at home. Occasionally, I would still see something and think, *Charlie would like that.* My impulse was to buy it, but I had to resist. We were still doing time inside the walls.

As a child, I had done time until I was old enough to wear makeup, but I knew I could eventually wear makeup. I had done time until I was old enough to drive, but I knew I would be able to drive one day. I had done time until I was married, until I had a child, another child, and so on. Now I was doing time with my dearly beloved in prison. I could not seem to get beyond wanting his release and a normal life for us to happen.

Charlie would not allow himself to ponder it. He had been inside for a long time and truly lived each day as it came. How would I come to peace? Would I ever automatically think about this day only that God had given me? Charlie gently coached me again and again in how to do this. He said, "There is just nothing we can do about it."

When we first talked about getting married, his greatest concern had been that I would not be able to learn to live with his incarceration forever. Now I was battling with that very issue.

The week before Easter that year, I attended a small group meeting at Ray and Pat's house. While we were in prayer, I thought, *Give up the dream of being together at home with Charlie. It is not fair to you and not fair to Charlie.* As I thought about this, I felt it was from the Lord, although we were never sure. As I spoke it, my voice took on a wail coming from the bottom of my feet and out my mouth. Later someone told me he had never heard such a cry of despair as my wail that night. People around me were compassionate and at the same time devastated alongside me that night. Graciously they prayed.

I kept going but was lethargic toward the Lord. *What could possibly be better than Charlie coming home, Lord?* But I was still not ready to give up, and He knew it. And the Lord would help me in some very real ways.

Chapter 27
COFFEE AND A DATE

A marriage in prison sometimes seems wedged between the guard's shout of "Visits" and "Visits over." But even that was leaving us. It was getting so hard for Charlie to get dressed in the morning, walk over to the visits building, and go through before-and-after strip searches that he often couldn't make it. Now I was also forced to miss a few visits, with the flu keeping me down. I was walking with a cane because of painful knee problems, a cane I was thankfully able to stop using when I started on an almost all-vegetable routine. Time together was becoming dearer.

By October of 2008, we learned Charlie was facing a partial or full amputation of his foot. Degeneration of his foot bones was causing extreme pain. Although he knew amputation surgery was coming up, he was not told when for security reasons. So we waited.

One day early in December, I arrived for a leisurely two-visit day, one in the morning, lunch with a friend, and one in the afternoon.

"Kay, come with me," the officer said when I entered the lobby, sparking a little fear in my heart. Hadn't we done this before?

My escort took me to the infirmary. *Charlie must have had his operation,* I reasoned, trying not to let apprehension cloud the anticipation of seeing my husband. No matter how I tried, I still found it disconcerting to arrive and find my husband had had a major medical incident and I had not been informed. Added to that, I would only be able to see him one hour instead of two, because infirmary visits were limited to one hour and required a personal guard for me in addition to the one required for the infirmary. If we had seen each other in the visit room, we would have shared the same two guards as the rest of the visitors.

This time, Charlie's bright yellow medical-wing room looked like a real hospital room of sorts. It had a wall-mounted TV and a normal hospital bed. Charlie asked me how to work the remote because he had never used one. The room was larger than the last one and had a tray table on wheels. He had somehow moved from a room that looked like a cell to a room that really looked like a hospital.

Charlie was wearing a gray sweatshirt and his orange pants, required by the prison for outside travel. I knew he had been outside. I could see his Bible on the nightstand by the bed. His foot was wrapped in bandages, and he smiled and nodded toward it. He was packed in here for a while. I leaned over and kissed him fiercely as if to hold back hearing about the obvious next step in his health decline.

"They took one toe and part of the side of my foot," he said with no emotion.

"Oh, okay. How are you feeling?"

His face was drawn as if in pain, but as always, he put forth a cheery smile. "I'm okay," he replied. "I take a bunch of pain medicine. Hate being here, though."

Okay, I thought. He is not really with it. Did he think he could be at the pod with this much medicine?

"Why?" I queried.

"Well, the last time I was here, Tiny could come and visit me, so the day passed a little faster. Now someone did something stupid, so no more visits from my pod." He was quiet for a second. "You know this is where the prison keeps men who are dying." I did not want to handle that thought.

Charlie was reclining in a large chair with a coffee in his hand, and I was given one of the institutional plastic chairs that were everywhere in the prison and placed just across from him. His height was still overwhelming to the large recliner chair, almost as if he could not really be sick. We were being watched by a guard, who sat no more than a foot behind me in another institutional plastic chair, reminding me of a school's desk-behind-a-desk arrangement.

Then came the colossal surprise. A wonderful woman guard who often worked in the infirmary came in and asked, "Kay, do you want a coffee?"

"Yes, I would love that."

The words were hardly out of my mouth when it struck me. I would soon be having my first "coffee date" with Charlie!

"Charlie, I cannot believe we are having a cup of coffee together," I said. The two guards laughed. The coffee was not like Dunks, but the idea of drinking our first cup together brought tears to my eyes.

"Yup, that's nice," he replied. "Hope it doesn't cost me too much." That's my man. Good with a quick zing. We laughed. But I knew this silliness was to soften the uneasiness we both had about him losing part of his body.

In the path the Lord had laid for us, having coffee together was huge. I also thought, *It could have been worse. They did not take his whole foot.* Charlie had always said, "I would rather they cut off my foot because the pain is so fierce at times." But even he was glad that the surgery had not been that extensive.

Later that evening, I called my daughter. "Saw Charlie today. He had a partial foot amputation. They let me go to the infirmary to visit him. Oh, and we had a cup of coffee together. Can you even imagine?"

"Mom, I don't want you going too fast with this guy," she said. Another laugh to ease the tension.

Meanwhile, I had called and met with my local representative to see about putting in a bill to return parole to Maine. For me, Charlie's illness seemed to be tied to asking for parole. Somehow I hoped it would remind people that there was a huge problem with the elderly in prison. Especially those who were no longer a danger to society.

About ninety days after Charlie's amputation, my phone rang. Because of my hearing problems, I don't get many calls. People all know e-mail is easier for me, and they do not call without reason. As I picked up the phone and flipped it open, I noticed it was from the prison. I listened to the machine tell me it was an inmate from Maine State Prison and I could hang up if I did not want to accept this call. I pressed 0 to accept it.

"Hi, Kay, it's Tiny."

Hmm. It was a blessing to have him call, but Tiny called only if Charlie could not call himself.

"My news is not so good. Charlie was taken to the outside hospital last night, and he was in a lot of pain."

"Oh, no." My stomach flipped with the news. "Where is he?"

"He's at Pen Bay."

After Tiny explained how to get the okay to go see Charlie, we said good-bye. The next morning I called the prison to get permission. The shift commander told me to go on over. I just had to notify the officers who were with Charlie in the hospital when I arrived. I grabbed a coat and keys and dashed out of the house.

Why don't they make an exception for someone who went to a hospital and call me? I wondered. *Why does Tiny have to do their job? Charlie always does as he should. He doesn't buck the system. Here it is again: the people in prison need to be kept separate in every way because they are so dangerous. It never occurs to them to consider he might be corrected!*

I needed to keep moving since it was already later in the day than my usual visit. The trip was going to be a bit longer than traveling to the prison. This would be a new experience, seeing Charlie outside the walls for the first time, and I knew I would have to follow every known rule since it was different from seeing him in our usual setting.

What would he look like outside the prison? Would he be wearing leg irons? How would that work on someone with a partial foot amputation? Could I be there for him? I just wanted to be there to hug him.

Two-and-a-half hours later, I drove down the decline into the parking lot at the Pen Bay hospital. Then I called the room to say I was coming up. They gave me the okay. I knew Charlie had been outside the walls several times for medical attention, but I had never been with him for one of these trips. Even his partial amputation was a day trip, not like this, overnight. At least with the infirmary visit behind me, I knew what he looked like in orange.

At the front desk, I had to get directions. He had been rushed to emergency and then into the Special Care Unit, Pen Bay's version of ICU.

"The Special Care Unit is right down this hall. Go in the waiting room and call on the phone there," a volunteer directed me.

To see him, I first had to enter a waiting room and then call from the phone inside. I knew they would have to screen me with extra security measures but did not know what those security measures would be.

It was odd, the waiting room. It was totally empty of people and quite dark. There was a lamp on in the middle of the day, and it did not give off much light. The phone was there, and a bunch of directions were written next to it for the families of the patients. Oh, how I dreaded talking by machine on crucial calls! Mechanical devices impair my hearing more. I picked up the phone.

"Special Care Unit, how may I help you?" chirped a cheerful nurse. Phew, I understood her.

"I am here to see Charlie Page."

"Hmm, Charlie Page. We don't have a Charlie Page."

"Charles Page?"

"No. No Charles Page."

"I just talked to someone in his room, and he is here."

"Well, no one is listed," she said.

On a guess, I ventured, "He is a prisoner."

"Oh, the prisoner. Yes, come in." The conversation reminded me of a grave I once saw behind the place where the old prison had stood in Thomaston. It has a granite marker with the number 26951 and the word "died" on it. Not even a name! I was so struck by the lack of a name or date of death on a tombstone. How could a life marker be placed without so much as a name? Charlie was here in the Special Care Unit, and they did not have so much as his name on their list. Only the fact that he was a prisoner was pertinent. I knew what Charlie would say to that. He would be telling me, "That is just the way it is."

I reached his room. There he was, my dearest Charlie, and he was struggling to breathe. With a pink blanket up around his neck, he was hunched up on his side huddling for warmth. There was a breathing tube under his nose. The monitors were hooked up, taking all sorts of measurements. On the whiteboard they had listed his sugar count and blood pressure the last time he was checked. *Okay. I can do this,* I thought. I took a breath. I was vaguely aware of officers in the room.

"Hi, Charlie," I said, touching his shoulder to get his attention. He could not catch his breath, but he knew I was there. I hugged him, and he responded with a weak smile.

Turning to the officers, I said, "Hi. I don't know what rules are here, but just tell me what to do."

One officer explained the rules. "Just hang your coat in the closet. Leave your purse there too. Don't get in the way of the medical people. You have to sit on that side of his bed." He pointed to the far side of the room.

Then the other guy offered, "Mrs. Page, we know you are not going to do anything, but we have to follow procedure." That was kind.

"Yes, I understand. I'm just grateful to be here with Charlie." And I was. And I was blessed that the guards seemed to care about my husband. Their compassion was a bright light for me right then. We did not know it then, but we were going see a lot of kindness among the guards. Some staff at the prison really are concerned. Charlie had said once, "Some people work in a prison because they *really* care about a human being who got himself into a terrible mess. Some are here because they would be inside prison otherwise." These guys cared.

The officers quickly found me a chair and showed me exactly where to sit. I had to be on the window or back side of the room. They needed to be by the door the room in case Charlie tried to escape. In Kosovo the seat of honor in Evan's house was on the back side of the room and across from the door so I could see who was coming in for my protection. That way I could escape. I understood war strategies. Now, we were stuffed into this small room with me on one side of the bed and two officers on the other side. One carried a gun. That shocked me. Not once had I seen a gun at the prison. In fact, I had not seen a gun since Kosovo.

Security is different outside the walls, I thought. *Like being in a war zone.*

An endless stream of doctors, nurses, and other medical personnel also squeezed in and out to do their work. I was content to sit anywhere they put me as long as I could be with Charlie in these horrific circumstances.

Charlie was wearing a typical hospital johnny. At least he was not in leg irons. That made sense, since his foot was the problem. God is merciful.

They called this section Special Care, but the name was not fooling me; it was a place for those in grave danger. Charlie's condition was critical. He had been there for several hours, and his breathing remained weak and labored. More time passed, and my fears were getting in my way. I was worried about the diagnosis, which was severe infection along with blood sugar troubles. It was startling because they had done the amputation and I had thought that fixed his problems. And the wealth of machines hooked up to his body, more than anything, were fear inspiring. That was my precious husband lying there.

Please heal him, Lord. Help him to breathe. As most people do who have someone hooked up to machines, I started to breathe for him. In and out.

The doctor told Charlie, "You have a severe infection in your whole body. We are giving you massive antibiotics."

To me he said, "He will have to take antibiotics for the rest of his life."

My head was swimming. I hugged Charlie and rubbed his frail hand, and he slept a lot. The next day, he seemed to respond to the medicine. His breathing became steadier. At one point he opened his eyes and said, "I think I have been here all night. Feeling better now."

"Yeah, right," I countered.

Nurses provided tender care and cheerful words for Charlie. Many did a double take at me, seeing "the prisoner" with an obviously loving woman visiting him. One nurse told me later that she wished more wives of prisoners would come visit their husbands because it helped the healing process. She had no idea just how difficult it was for the family of a high-security prisoner to come and see him even in the prison if he was sick.

He was released back to the prison when they felt he was ready. Shortly, we were off and running with a bill in the Maine State Legislature to help unhealthy older inmates by bringing back parole. We hoped to get relief for long-term inmates with debilitating illnesses and who were no longer any danger to anyone. Our bill was going to be heard at the Criminal Justice Committee. Many people e-mailed, wrote, and called, and we talked to various state representatives and senators.

Oh, how real it was to me, the need for parole for the older inmates, as I juggled hospital visits with planning for the hearing! The hearing was seven days after Charlie went back to the prison from Pen Bay. Hearing day came and went, and the committee decided not to vote it out to the House because it would be unconstitutional. Only the governor has the right to change the length of a sentence. We were not asking to change the length of the sentence, just where the sentence would be served, and just for those who were no longer a threat. The hearing is vivid in my memory because my head was swimming with concerns over Charlie's illness.

Three days after the hearing, Charlie was admitted again to the hospital for the second or third time that year. When I called the captain, he said I could go see Charlie anytime he was taken to an outside hospital for treatment. This was a long stay as they tried to stabilize him. As is normal, I wanted to go to the hospital every day to see my husband, but the drive was long. Often I had to stop on the way home and take a power nap in the parking lot of a store to get me safely back.

Two days into this stay in the hospital, I arrived when the officers were ordering lunch for Charlie and themselves. One of them, familiar with how the hospital treated visitors, asked me, "Kay, do you want to order lunch too? Other families do that here. It's called guest lunch."

"Of course," I said. I laughed. "Wow, Charlie, we are on an expensive date here. No more just coffee, but we are sitting down to lunch together! I am not sure Camelia would approve of us moving into this next stage of our relationship."

"She'll just have to get used to it," he grinned back with a twinkle in his eye, obviously feeling better. Even the officers laughed. Another milestone in our marriage—having a meal together. God had heard my plea.

When the meals came, I helped set Charlie's and my food on the same hospital tray. We settled back and started lunch together. He gave a wink and a slight smile. All was well for us.

By early April, Charlie was still at the hospital and I was staying up in Thomaston with our dear friends Harry and Elaine from Kairos. Early each morning I called in to let the officers know I was coming for still another visit. Already on my way to the hospital, I just needed to call the room. The captain had said to go in anytime; just call before I got there.

Guards are under orders, and the fellow who answered the phone in Charlie's room told me I could only visit for one hour. The officers had been pretty helpful up until this time, but now the officers with Charlie had changed. I was shocked, because Charlie was so ill and there had been so many days for him in an outside hospital. He had serious complications with diabetes.

I called a friend in the legislature to tell her what was going on. "Kay, I think they will let you stay longer. I'll find out," she said.

A short time later, my friend called back. "Kay, they will let you stay longer. I called the commissioner, who called the warden, who called the assistant warden, who called the captain, who called the security sergeant, who called the officers in Charlie's room. Those officers said 'fine' to the sergeant, who called back the captain, who called back the assistant warden, who called back the warden, who called back the commissioner. Then the commissioner called me to say it was all taken care of."

If she was trying to cheer me up, she succeeded. I laughed at the way she put it, thinking what a wonderful children's picture book her statement would make. My heart began to beat again, but she still did not know how long I could stay. Someone would call soon with that information.

A few minutes later a deputy warden called me to see if what she had arranged was good for me. "Kay, I got three hours for your visits. How does that sound?" she asked.

I decided to be honest. "Well, thanks so much, but that is not really great. When Charlie is in the hospital, he goes for tests, sometimes X-rays, or has to get medical procedures and all, so five hours would be more toward normal. People in the hospital are comforted by family being there with them. If he were home, I would be camping out overnight, like most wives. Just because he is in prison does not mean that I am any less concerned about my ailing husband."

The assistant commissioner was an especially kind person, just not used to arranging things like this. She listened to me, and she *heard* me.

"Okay," she said. "I will get word to them that you can visit for five hours after you arrive there." I was so thankful that she could see beyond the traditional thinking and listen to my reasoning! To most staff of the Department of Corrections, I was just a prisoner's wife, about as insignificant as a prisoner. This lady treated me as any family member with problems.

When I got there, the officer had written in the logbook that I was allowed a five-hour visit, and he said, "Kay, you can stay for five hours. They called to change that one-hour thing."

In due time, Charlie was moved to a regular room for recovery and monitoring. With deep gratitude, I was able to tend to some of his needs in the hospital. A nurse's aide came into the room one morning wanting to put lotion on his legs, which were alligator bumpy and like red leather. His legs were swollen all out of proportion. Someone had drawn lines on them with a marker to show eventual progress in lessening the swelling. Looking at me, the woman's eyes lit up, and she asked, "Do you want to put the lotion on your husband's legs?" It seemed like she knew a wife putting on lotion would work toward the healing of a patient. I looked to one officer, and he nodded okay.

"I would love to," I said. It was a pleasure to be able to do so. Another answer to my plea to the Lord. But it served to point out even more the little things we missed as husband and wife.

"Charlie, do you mind if I put lotion on those sorry legs of yours?" I asked. He smiled in reply.

Although this got to be a regular thing that year, I managed to mess it up one time. I grabbed a bottle of what I thought was lotion and rubbed it in well. It was shampoo. Had I rubbed dangerous chemicals into his precarious system?

"Don't know if I ought to be letting you do this again," Charlie quipped.

What time we had between the pokes, prods, meds, and X-rays, we spent looking out the window at the wildlife. The room was at ground level, and I loved having Charlie tell me which bird was what, pointing out their habits along the way. When he was stabilized, he went back to the prison.

In May, my local representative, John Tuttle, wanted to get me into the governor's office to discuss Charlie's condition after the defeat of the parole bill. John felt that it was cruel to have an elderly man not able to have proper food and care when he had diabetes. He sincerely believed the governor would care too. So we squeezed in a visit there.

That day we met with the governor's aide, and she added to my frustration. She was droning on about the governor, and then she went into Charlie and "the nature of his crime," apparently not knowing that he was a person. I knew that his crime was horrible, but his crime would never change. *He* had changed. Clemency means mercy, and she did not seem merciful. Obviously, it is called the Department of Corrections because someone along the line believed people could change, but I guess this lady and the governor did not.

Still hoping to get beyond this woman to see the governor, John began to describe Charlie's illness. "He is an old man. He has diabetes and had a partial amputation. He's been in prison for many years and has been hospitalized a lot this spring."

With ice in her voice she stated, "Charlie is fine."

"You are not qualified to determine Charlie's health," he countered.

"The assistant commissioner said he is a lot better," she said.

John patiently pointed out, "She is not a qualified medical person. She cannot make that determination."

For the rest of that spring and into the summer, Charlie had troubles with medical problems. One day he was hungry at visits and told me they were giving him Cheetos to keep him stable with his sugar. But they were not giving him good greens or fruit to help his health overall. A doctor in late April had told him he did not have to be seen. Meanwhile, a suspicious death had occurred at the prison, causing extra tension inside the walls and in families. One day in June, Charlie went after visits to see the doctor and was told he could not be seen until the next day— but the next day he was taken out to Pen Bay for a day because he was so sick. Two days later, back at the prison, he asked a nurse to see the doctor, and the nurse said no. His visit to a foot doctor in Bangor was canceled because the prison did not have enough guards to escort him. Ten days later he was taken out of work in the wood shop because he had a silver-dollar-sized ulcer on his heel. Now he was in a wheelchair. Shortly after, he was hospitalized again for three days for wound care. It seemed they did not understand cause and effect. To ignore something caused greater problems and incurred a larger cost.

Meanwhile, I tried to call his social worker and then a woman who was appointed to share medical information with me. This circular web of sickness and lack of care was deeply frustrating. In early August we had a reprieve from hospitals for about ten days after John Tuttle and I attempted to meet with the governor—and then I heard my phone ring as I was sitting down to do e-mail.

"Please press zero," came the voice command to hook me up to the call from Maine State Prison. I could not understand who the inmate was. My heart was racing, wondering if it was Charlie with a nice hello or Tiny with a message. Finally I understood. It was Tiny.

"Kay, more bad news for you. Charlie was rushed back to the hospital again, and he was totally out of it when he left the pod."

Again I called the prison for permission for a visit. Charlie must have still been in transport because the captain could not tell me anything. At last I got the word from the captain that I could go up. I was not at all prepared for what was next.

I walked in to still another hospital room reserved for my husband. I happened to glance at the bed before I greeted Charlie. At first I thought I was seeing things. I actually touched it before I was sure. To my shock, I saw his infected foot bound with cuff and a chain secured to the end of the bed.

"*What* is this?" I almost roared, pointing to the restraint.

Even in his pain, Charlie did not miss my anger boiling up. "Don't worry, Dear. That is okay. I can barely feel it. It is regulation to have them on." He was quite practiced at keeping calm in front of staff, carrying out the protocol for prisoners even when he was upset. I was learning to suppress my feelings inside the jurisdiction of the walls; wearing leg irons was a regulation. But it did seem beyond common decency considering the nature of his condition.

During that day I watched, trying to hide my horror, as doctors and nurses worked on Charlie, taking samples carefully from his infected foot around the cuff on his leg. A nurse had kindly put cloths between his skin and the metal. She could not judge the care the prison was giving or if Charlie was dangerous still. He remained chained to the hospital bed that day.

The next day I breathed a sigh of relief at seeing the restraints were gone. I touched his gentle face, and we never mentioned it again. With the chains off, the hospital felt like a place of healing again. The sun was a merry gold, lighting the room that morning, melting away my frustrations with the prison rules.

But the journey was far from over. Adding to our sense of hopelessness with the medical care at the prison, a letter of refusal from the Clemency Board arrived. There were the words again: he did not "demonstrate a compelling and appropriate need for clemency." My heart raced when I read those words again, after all the hospital visits with serious enough relapses to land him in an ICU so many times already that year. What in the world was a compelling and appropriate reason?

My heart felt worn out at this point. As I stop to reflect, I do not know how we kept going, but our love was rooted so deeply that now the thought of giving up never crossed my mind. I finally knew I could never abandon Charlie and he would never abandon me. His body was failing and I thought I might lose him, but our hearts toward each other were healed from two lifetimes of rejection. To God be the glory. And in the midst of all the turmoil, God was about to send a wonderful blessing.

Chapter 28

BLESSINGS

Ⅰn my life with Charlie, the August hospital visit with the leg-chain was the most difficult time for me so far. But the Lord didn't leave us without a blessing. In balance, this is what the Lord did in another hospital incident, this one in the September.

Arriving at the prison for a visit at the usual time, I watched as the lobby gradually filled with people who were going to visit that morning. Families of people in prison have a guarded anticipation for seeing their loved one. Guarded because almost anything can happen to delay or cancel the visit. This time, a captain with near-perfect posture came over and pulled me aside to say I would not be going in just yet.

"Kay. Stay here in the lobby. I will come tell you what is going on in a little while," he said.

Charlie had called from the prison late in the week and said he was not feeling well. Rules are such that I could not know when he was in transit. But for us delays had happened so many times that I sensed that Charlie was in transit for medical care at the hospital and that was the holdup.

The other visitors went through the two metal detectors, with the usual stopping for someone's belt, shoes with a metal shank in them, or a necklace made of metal. Many turned toward me with sympathetic eyes, knowing that Charlie was probably sick again. Soon they had disappeared down the hall toward the sally port. I was happy for them, but anxious as I waited to hear about Charlie.

I chatted with the officer at the desk, looked out on the parking lot at the goings-on out there, and paced around the room. Almost two hours later, the captain returned. He said Charlie had been taken to the hospital that morning, and I could not see him because he was in emergency. I wanted to hurry to his side, but I knew I could not see him if he was being treated in an ER. In a "normal" situation I would have to wait outside emergency all night to see my husband. But due to security procedures, I might not be able to visit even then. I decided to go home and travel the 120 miles to the hospital at the start of a new day.

Lord, it is Your problem.

I prayed as much as I could. Too often I just jumped into fear and did not do what was needed until time passed. I could hear Charlie saying, "There is just nothing you can do about it." It was his wisdom telling me this.

As hard as it was in the beginning, it was on the weekend during that September hospital stay that we received our crown jewel moment after four years of marriage. I had been staying with Harry and Elaine again. Harry is a minister. This Saturday he was preparing for the next day's service, and he mentioned that he needed to get his minister's robe to wear for the celebration. The question ran through my head, *Could Harry give us communion in the hospital later in the day since he is an area pastor?*

"Harry, do you go into Pen Bay to minister to people in the hospital? Could you come and give communion to Charlie and me tomorrow if the prison will allow it?"

"Of course," he said. My tears started immediately, not even knowing if it would happen. Harry had previously had a security clearance to go into the prison to preach at services there, so it was a possibility.

"Harry, this will be the first time Charlie and I have shared communion together if it happens. They would not allow it at our wedding." I knew he was moved by what I said the next morning—he had never thought about how important receiving communion together would be to those getting married inside the walls. I could hear him singing a little tune as he prepared to go to his church. He was willing to do anything to facilitate communion for us.

Sitting at the Dunkin' Donuts parking lot that morning, I called the shift commander to ask permission. My phone did not work at Harry and Elaine's house. I wanted so much for this to happen.

"Captain, this is Kay Page, and I would like to visit Charlie again this morning."

"Of course," he replied. "How is he doing?"

"As well as possible," I said. "I have something else to ask you."

"What?"

"Charlie and I have never had communion together. I am staying with Pastor Harry and Elaine Harrigan. Harry is a minister. He said he would bring communion to us if the prison was okay with it." I quickly added, "Harry is already approved by the prison. He does services there." I held my breath.

"Oh, that is fine with me," the captain said, and I breathed out a sigh of deep relief.

"One more thing," I said, hoping he would not change his mind with still another request. "What should he bring? Bread in a wrapper? Juice with a cap still on?"

"No, tell him to just bring it the way he would to anyone in the hospital."

Oh, Lord, this is too good to be true. Thank You.

I called Harry and related the good news. Sure enough, at two o'clock that afternoon Harry came and brought communion to us, offering it to the guards as well. My tears started when Harry opened the door to the hospital room and did not stop until he was on his way back out the door. Charlie and I had wanted to receive communion together, and with the help of a good captain, the Lord granted us the desire of our hearts. What a blessing. We held hands the whole time, hearing the comforting old words of communion new for us at that moment. "Take this bread in remembrance of Me, My body broken for you. Take this fruit of the vine, My blood poured out for you."

Communion received at a wedding has special meaning for a husband and wife, but after all these years, through all the illness and loss, that breaking of bread remains a hallmark of our life together, a remembrance of how Christ gave His all for these two raggedy people who fell in love one day inside the walls.

In October Charlie was admitted to a hospital in Belfast. They suspected pneumonia. He was also being treated for COPD and renal downturn. Difficult diagnoses were being considered, and Charlie was on so many drugs that I could not keep up. One morning we were just talking with two kind guards, looking for a break from the serious nature of Charlie's illness. Charlie was already in orange for the trip back to the prison, but he had not been discharged yet.

"How do you keep the public from panicking when you take Charlie out dressed in his orange outfit?" I asked one guard. I had to leave before they packed up Charlie for travel back to the prison, so I had never seen him actually leave.

"Well, we sometimes put Charlie on a gurney and cover the orange. We put a blanket right up to his chin to hide the chains and the orange suit. Just leave his whiskers out." This ridiculous picture made us all laugh until tears came, but I did not know if they were pulling my leg or not. Charlie did not mention if this had ever really happened to him, and his belly laugh was louder than anyone's.

At that very moment a new nurse walked in, and merriment burst forth still again as we all turned at the same time to see who was there. A woman was in scrubs that were the exact color of orange that Charlie wore for travel. It was a well-timed entrance, and finally we managed to stop guffawing long enough for someone to say, "We are not laughing at you, but your scrubs are the exact orange of the suit Charlie has to wear when he travels." That particular hospital was not used to having prisoners come for treatment. No one was used to Charlie and me laughing over the situation. But how could we help it?

Not all things were as uplifting. In late October I had a meeting with the corrections commissioner and two state representatives, including Charlie's advocate, John Tuttle. I wanted to go over Charlie's diet with them, and John had arranged the meeting. As soon as Charlie got out of the hospital, a doctor at the prison had told him he could never have a renal diabetic diet. It was too complicated. I wanted to talk to the commissioner about this.

When we all arrived in Augusta, the meeting began. I talked for a while about the problems, and they were aware of his many hospital stays. One of the representatives entered in with the part of the conversation she and the commissioner had in mind.

"Kay, we have some good news for you. Tell her," she directed the fellow who headed the DOC.

"Kay," he began, "Charlie will be one of the fifteen or so people in the state to be put on medical home release. It is for people with serious and life-threatening medical problems and who are no longer any danger to society."

"Oh," was all I could think to say. After so many disappointments, this was startling. Was this true? Was it really going to happen?

"Do you like that idea, Kay?" he asked. "Charlie will have to fill out some papers for this to happen. It will probably take until the first of the year."

"Yes, of course," I managed.

The commissioner was dressed in casual Maine, a plaid jacket over a white shirt. Charlie had told me that he had worked for this man and admired him. He wanted the best for the prisoners. But my thoughts went back to our time of wondering, when Charlie had seen a paper with "Probation?" instead of the usual "Murder One—Life" on it. Nothing had ever been said about that again, and like many hopes and happenings, it was left hanging. Of course there was no proof of Charlie ever seeing and signing that paper. Would this be the same thing? Would we once again be left hanging with this vague promise?

But I was here to hear the promise as well as John. My heart tentatively started to hope.

I was cautiously happy that there was such a thing. I jotted myself a note to tell Charlie that he would have to fill out some medical forms again. Finally, from the man who would know, I had received the best news of our lives. But like me, Charlie was suspicious.

Charlie was admitted again to the hospital in November. As soon as I knew, I called the shift commander before I left home at 8 a.m. Reeling with dread, I managed to make it to the parking lot.

"Sure, Mrs. Page. Go right up there," the captain said.

"Thanks," I replied before hanging up.

Been through this drill before, I thought. *Easy.*

When I arrived there after traveling 120 miles, the officer told me, "Mrs. Page, you will have to leave by 1 p.m." It was 10:30 in the morning.

"Why?" I asked. "I have been approved for five-hour visits."

"The captain said he did not know anything about five-hour visits."

I did not argue, knowing it would do no good. This way I could spend what time we did have in quality time with my husband.

While Charlie and I caught up on things, one officer was going through the logbook, reading every page. I thought he must be catching up on all the visits Charlie and I had had. There had been so many. Running his finger down each page, he was searching diligently for something.

In the middle of deep conversation, Charlie and I were startled when the officer interrupted to say, "I just saw where it is noted that you may have five-hour visits. I will call the captain and see what he says. Can't promise anything."

What a blessing when he got off the phone saying, "The captain is sorry for the mix-up, and you can stay for five hours." What humble men those two were—one who took the time to search the pages and pages of the logbook and one who apologized for the problem. I have heard plenty of stories about the officers and captains who do terrible things to the men inside, but in fairness, I've met some who are gems of human kindness.

December arrived, and still another call saying Charlie had been taken to the hospital. To hear he was so sick again was discouraging, even more so because it was the holidays. Our prayer was that Charlie would not be there over Christmas. His amputation had been in December of 2008, and it had been an extremely long year. The Lord said yes to our request, and Charlie was soon released from the hospital. We hoped he could leave the prison quickly on the home confinement the commissioner had promised. Still, Christmas came and went with no more word on that front.

In January I happened to see the woman representative who was with the commissioner and asked when we could expect the home confinement to happen. "Oh, Kay, these things take time," she said. "I really don't know."

Later in the spring I attended a conference in Portland put on by the NAACP and the commissioner about working together to make prisons better for prisoners and families. I was the Maine representative for CURE (Citizens United to Rehabilitate Errants), a grassroots organization to help inmates and their families. The woman representative was there and of course the commissioner, as well as my NAACP friends. I waited awhile, thinking maybe they would talk about this new thrust to get elderly sick people into home confinement. It would obviously be a great way to work with those inside and their families, as well as a place for the state to save some money. Warehousing prisoners is expensive, and Maine had the highest expenses per prisoner of any state.

Finally I went up to the commissioner, who seemed to be avoiding eye contact. I asked how many had gone out on home confinement and when it would be Charlie's turn. "It's illegal," he said.

"Why?" I asked, having read the regulations online again and again about supervised home confinement. Maine permits the commissioner to send someone home if the director of medical care has determined the prisoner has a terminal or severely incapacitating condition and that care outside the facility is medically appropriate. Hospice can be done in the home. If anyone needed outside care for sheer number of hospitalizations, it was Charlie.

"It is just illegal," he said, and he looked relieved that someone asked him something else.

I went over to the woman representative who was sitting in one of the auditorium chairs right down front. "The commissioner says home confinement is illegal. The regulations I read online said the commissioner could order medical home confinement at his discretion." I was trying my best to stay calm and focused.

"I don't know, Kay. I will have to look into it and get back to you." At that moment I knew this was yet another rabbit trail, and we would never again hear about home confinement for those with serious medical problems who were no longer a danger to society. Still another dead end. We would learn to live with the medical arrangements inside the prison.

Doing time was hard for both of us.

Chapter 29
OUR LAST SPRING

A bizarre call came after two more years of medical stress and hospitalizations for Charlie, in February 2012. A strange voice told me to press something on my phone, but it did not sound like a call from the prison. With hearing problems, I thought it was Charlie calling, and I pushed the usual zero on my phone to connect the call. It then said, "You have refused this call." What I was expecting was, "Your call has been connected." I sensed something was wrong, but no one had called from the prison, not even Tiny. I called the main number of the prison to inquire about Charlie.

"We don't know where he is," came their startling response. Now, I was pretty sure the highest security prison in Maine knew where their high-security prisoners were, especially someone in close security. If Charlie had not been so ill all the time, I would have laughed. After a few other tries on the phone for information, I decided to drive to the prison. The captain would probably okay me to go to the hospital if Charlie was there. Actually, I was so concerned about his health that the drive seemed a small price to pay to find out what was going on.

Two-and-a-half hours later, the captain came toward me in the prison lobby. "I have someone from Medical coming up to talk to you. Charlie is in the hospital. You cannot visit him because he is having an operation right now. Plan on seeing him tomorrow."

"Okay."

Done with the captain, I was ready for the medical people who were coming to talk to me.

"Hi, Kay." The man reached out to shake my hand. "I am the head of Medical Services here, and Charlie is having an amputation. I have been on the phone with the hospital, but they could not tell me if Charlie's amputation was a toe, a foot, or his leg."

Why the highest security prison in the state, with a big medical staff, could not get pertinent information on one of their prisoners was beyond me. What was happening to Charlie?

On the way out, I saw the captain again. He said, "And you do know he is at Maine Med? Call me after 6 a.m. and I will okay your visit."

Well, no, nobody mentioned Maine Med. I would have stopped there instead of driving all the way to Warren.

Next morning I called the captain, who said, "Charlie is having dialysis to get ready for the operation. I will call when I hear something."

"He did not have the operation yesterday?"

"No."

Late that afternoon the fellow from Medical called, saying, "Charlie had his foot amputated, so call the captain in the morning for a visit." With no small struggle over not knowing *major* things about my husband's medical condition until after they happened, I hung up the phone.

Finally surviving three days of red tape while trying to get a visit with Charlie, I was let in. He looked rough.

"Honey, I tried to call you before they took my foot, but could not get through. I really wanted to talk to you." That was the strange call I had received and managed to refuse. I could see on his face it had been hard alone. "I have to have dialysis now because of the amputation. I will be having it three days a week, I think. I had it before and after the operation." Charlie had a staggering amount of medical news for me. Now he would be on dialysis all the time.

"They said maybe I could be on a transplant list, but I doubt it," he said. "We will not be having as many visits because I have to leave the prison early to be there for dialysis. Somewhere near the prison is all I know. We will have to figure it out."

I nodded. Charlie and I had not had a lot of visits recently, and the prison had changed the visits anyway. I could no longer go any day that Charlie and I wanted.

He was in a lot of pain, phantom pain. "This is the worst pain I ever had," he told me. "And it is real strange because it is worst in my foot. The one I lost." I was less mystified by that than he was. Unlike me, Char-

lie had never read about amputations. I'd had the young man from
Afghanistan and had read a lot about it back then. And the kid had talked
about it.

"They are testing me to see if the doctor got all the poison. I may
have to have another operation on Sunday to take my leg. Don't know
how much."

My heart ached for my husband. He'd not only had a major operation that would restrict him more, but he'd had no loved one beside him
as he signed papers to okay it. All this was adding to the growing list of
reasons we could not see each other. And this time he was not joking
about them taking his leg.

"Let the kids talk about it again and again," I had been told as I
sought out strategies for helping traumatized kids in war countries. Now,
I was getting what the experts call secondary trauma from all that had
happened since I last saw my husband. And he needed to talk more. And
he needed me near. I would visit him every day if I was not stopped.

On Monday they amputated his leg to his knee, another major operation on a man already weak. The lead officer in his room said, "Kay, I
have been on twelve hours a day with Charlie. I even went into the operating room with him. We are staying down here in Portland because that's
easier than going back and forth each day." He was preaching to the choir.
I knew how long a drive it was to Warren.

I asked with a half-smile, "Did you really go into the operating room
with Charlie? What did you think he would do while under anesthesia?"

"It was Charlie I was protecting. You never know what a doctor or
nurse thinks of someone who is in prison. I was protecting him."

"Wow," I said. Thinking back, I am not sure if he was serious,
because he is a lot of fun. He was probably trying to get a smile out of
Charlie. The doctors were excellent and would not intentionally do anything dangerous to a patient. But I admired the officer who was either
protecting Charlie or trying to make us feel better.

It was also mentioned that Charlie would need a heart valve replace-
ment. I'd had one eight months before this, so I wondered how in the
world he would survive that. It had been hard on my body, and I was

relatively healthy. One thing at a time.

"You will need to have a tube inserted in your chest," a doctor told Charlie. "It will help when you start getting regular dialysis. The amputation caused the renal failure, but it can correct itself with good diet and good care." I doubted he would have the right food and care at the prison, as did Charlie. Experience had taught us otherwise. Due to an investigation by OPEGA into prison medical care, the prison would get a new medical provider in July, but July was a long way off. Once again, there was just nothing we could do about it.

Dialysis would be the next big hurdle. I was introduced seriously to the renal kidney diet, a very complicated way of eating. Just trying to get a diabetic diet had been difficult at the prison. Surely now they would let Charlie out on medical clemency!

A bid for Charlie's release was put in by some students at the University of Maine legal clinic. They had built an amazing case and had already sent it to the Clemency Board before the amputation. The board meeting was in April. It was almost March. The student now in charge was adding addenda for the board to see before the date of their meeting because so much had rapidly changed.

Charlie had received amazing aftercare at Maine Med. We could laugh and joke again as I came in early each day. He got healthier before my eyes. I dreamed of his being let out on medical clemency and continuing his recovery here.

But after Charlie was stabilized, the attending doctor told the two officers, "I just talked to the prison, and they assured me that they have all the equipment that is needed to get Charlie back in shape for his prosthesis.

"He could get off dialysis with excellent food. So he does not have to go to rehab in Portland." Well aware of the churning in my stomach that moment, I knew Medical at the infirmary probably could not even come close to doing rehab.

Finally back to the prison, our problem again became Charlie being allowed to see me. He could be pushed to the visit room in his wheelchair, but the doctor ordered him to stay in the infirmary. And someone was not allowing me to visit in the infirmary. Charlie thought it was the doctor, but we didn't know for sure.

April came and I was allowed to see him again, but now Charlie was worried about pain medication. He had always been afraid of overmedication because he had committed his crime while on prescribed meds. The urgency to bring him home was only growing.

Our current student lawyer had been astute, asked the right questions, and gathered the right information. We dared to think there was a good chance this time to get him home on a supervised home confinement. He finally had an obvious need to be out and at home or at least in a nursing home.

The Clemency Board convened in April, and they decided not to immediately say no to us, as they had done the last two times. The governor's lawyer called our student lawyer to convey this news. It was hard to say there was not a compelling reason for the governor to hear his case. It would be discussed again on July 19.

About mid-May Charlie wrote, "I am so happy to be going back to church and to the yard to work out with Mike." For the moment, things were looking up. But at the visit just a few days later, he said the doctor had restricted him again and he was not going to be allowed to go to the yard or visit. It had been three months of not being allowed to go to his pod and be with friends. I was able to write him every day so that he could get a feel for life outside the infirmary. Our visits were scarce, so he was feeling like he was in solitary with no one but officers and other patients around. It was a roller-coaster ride, moment by moment for both of us.

Toward the end of May, Charlie was allowed to come to visits once. He came in but was feeling really sick, and after twenty minutes he said he had to leave. He had always braved it out to close to the end before, so I knew he was terribly sick. My heart bled for him. *Charlie, why is this happening? I am so sorry for you.*

Oh my God in heaven, help us to walk in this. So many things seem so impossible. But all things are possible with You. Lord, help my dear Charlie, whatever is wrong.

Once again, I was to leave the prison in Warren with my heart aching, in tears and dismay about our lack of time together at a horrible juncture in his life. The drive home was no longer a time of prayer and worship to me. It had become a long trip home in tears.

Chapter 30
MORE AND MORE

A couple of days after that shortened visit, the phone rang. "Mrs. Page," a voice said, "Charlie has been hospitalized again. He was admitted a few days ago to Maine Medical in Portland."

"Thanks," I said, amazed. It was the first time I was *ever* notified by the prison that Charlie was in the hospital. I felt a mixture of joy that he was nearer home now and panic that they had called me. I knew this had to be serious. Was this the end? Charlie and I knew his health was not going well.

The caller wasn't done. "Oh, Kay, I also arranged a visit for you tomorrow. Just tell me what time you want to go in to see Charlie, and I will arrange it with the officer," she told me.

"I will be there at 9 a.m. Can you arrange that?"

"Sure can. And Charlie is now medium security. He will have Maine Correctional Facility officers with him. You will have to call them each day to arrange visits."

Whew. That was the strangest statement I had heard in ages. He now was not dangerous—officially? *All the better to scare me with,* I thought. For a period of time he was not quite as dangerous, I guess. Poor guy. But alone and extremely sick in a hospital far away, and I had not yet shown up.

I was grateful for everything, albeit a few days late. It had been such a nightmare trying to find him in February. And getting the news that he was having an amputation and that the medical department did not know what kind of amputation it was—that had been awful. No one had called me then. They could not even find him.

Tiny's niece faithfully called that night to tell me what I already knew. She had just gotten word about the hospital. But I felt strongly this was not good news.

When I called MCC in the morning they said I could visit him any-time, any day since he was now medium security. That also meant they only had to have one officer with him, a sensible move on their part. What danger could he possibly be in this condition?

And thus began our final journey together. Charlie was going down-hill fast, but he refused to see it that way. Once he got a mite better with good food and me coming to see him, his constant chatter was about getting back to the prison, and then getting a leg, and then getting back to work.

Each day there seemed to be something else wrong. He had a heart test and his hand was swollen. They cleaned his wrist out surgically and then did it again.

A social worker from the prison called me for the first time. She wanted to know how I was doing. In ten years of knowing Charlie, that had never happened. I was suspicious of all this attention. There was absolutely nothing I could do about it. So I went about the business of loving on Charlie. He got perked up again with decent food and care and went back to the prison *again*.

Ten days later, on June 18, he was admitted to Pen Bay and sent right back to Maine Med. But they did not let me know this time. On June 21 I went to Warren to visit him and found out he had been at Maine Med as I had driven by two hours previously. All alone and wondering where I was for four days. Can one heart break over and over again for a man?

"Go on right down there, Kay," the captain said.

When I got there, we could finally talk. "I had a heart attack the first day, and then on the second day too," Charlie told me.

"Your husband is getting better as he has the right food here. His liver is improving," a nurse said.

"I was out of it last night," Charlie continued. "And I can't see out of one eye." He held up his thin hand to try to see it. They had put in a pacemaker to revive him that night.

My middle son, Todd, who had met Charlie at the prison, brought his daughters to the hospital. Charlie was in pain but was very excited to meet the girls. Being very sick and nervous, he did not talk much to them, but I could see how grateful he was that someone would bring more grandchildren for him to meet. He had for years been convinced that the outside world hated people in prison, a partially true fear. This was a little interlude of joy for us both. I was very proud of Todd for bringing the girls. His family enjoyed my husband. And Charlie adored each one of them.

My daughter Tracey and her husband, Vincent, were coming in early July with their year-old twins. Charlie was beside himself with plans after having met the two lovely older girls. "What will I do if I am in the hospital and the twins come?" was his newest worry.

"I know they want the kids to meet you. Tracey and Vincent are concerned that they will never meet the guy who loves their grandma."

With the meeting of the Clemency Board and a possible decision about sending Charlie nearer home coming in July, I was also looking for the prison to give an okay to let Charlie come to a nursing home in Sanford. My own hometown doctor had bravely acquiesced when I asked him to take Charlie as a patient. He remarked, "This would be an interesting case." I was grateful for his sense of adventure. Records were sent to him as we continued to plan.

"John, can you get the nursing home to okay Charlie coming there?" I asked our state representative. John Tuttle had met Charlie many times and discovered that Charlie was indeed a changed man, not the man who had been so dangerous in the start of his life in prison. He referred to Charlie as his constituent. "I will get on it, Kay. Do you have the okay from your doctor here in Sanford?"

"Yes."

My planning went into overdrive. How would I fix the house if Charlie was allowed to visit from the nursing home? Knowing Charlie was pretty sick, I tried to do all I could so he would be moved right to a nursing home when they gave the word.

The day arrived for our youngest grandchildren to fly into Portland, and I went to see Charlie early before I had to be home to welcome them. It was nine days until the Clemency Board would again look at the petition and decide if the governor would hear us.

Charlie had an uncertain look when I got to the hospital room that day. "Sweetheart, I have some really bad news today. I only have a couple of days to a few weeks to live," he told me. I could see the anguish in his eyes at having to tell me. With others he always feigned bravado. With me his face was an open book.

Lord, help me. Keep my heart beating so I can be with Charlie.

Often calm when an earth rocker comes, I said, "Oh Charlie," and hugged him. We both well knew he would go to a place without pain and no prison walls. But parting would be hard for us.

It came to mind that God had given me a dream back in the spring of Charlie going. It was odd, because in the dream, Charlie was in a bed in the prison infirmary, dying. At the time, the new doctor at the prison would not let me visit Charlie in the infirmary. I had chosen to believe the dream was a nightmare, not a preparation from the Lord, because at the time I just could not face Charlie dying.

Now the reality was here. Charlie, the rugged independent woodsman, needed to talk now more than any time in his life. He could not be alone, nor could I.

But the tension began to show during this visit. We were discussing very stupid things. He wanted his blanket over him, and then he did not. I wanted to clean up the room and his bedside table, and he wanted me to sit and talk. Both of us were clinging to things to do in place of facing the inevitable. I finally relented and sat down to talk.

"We are at each other because of what they told me," he said. I agreed. And my daughter was due to arrive right after my visit was over that morning. "Will Tracey come still? Now that I am not going to live?" he beseeched.

"I am sure she will. But she will need to rest after the long trip with the kids, and the kids will need to get used to the new house," I explained. "I think they will rest tomorrow and come on Wednesday. I'll be in tomorrow while they sleep in. God will let you meet the kids. I am sure."

Charlie seemed to need assurance, being so weak. "Can Charlie's step-grandchildren come in to see him?" I asked the hospital staff. The kids were just over a year old, and I wondered if youngsters were allowed into the ICU. They were already on the list for the prison.

"Yes, as long as they are well behaved and not screaming. You will have to watch that they do not step on the floor or get on the bed of the patient. There are germs present with all the patients here."

Having an officer from a totally different prison in charge added to our complications. I assured him these two kids were on Charlie's visit list, and I knew he could easily check it with Maine State Prison. Busying himself with getting the names of those coming in soon would be difficult because the names were Bulgarian and hard for him to write down. From past experience I thought there might be a negative reaction to added visitors, but this fellow was pleasant and helpful.

Trust God, I kept telling myself. He was so carefully arranging things.

"They will come see Charlie at the hospital. The kids can come in. I checked. As long as they don't get screaming here in ICU," I told the guard.

"Okay. When will they come in?"

"I will be up here tomorrow, but they are probably too tired to come until Wednesday," I explained again. I guess he had not heard me tell Charlie.

"They can sleep in after the long ride with the year-old twins," I assured Charlie, who was listening. "Tracey and Vincent are anxious to see you too."

The previous September after my heart operation, seeing these twins had been my goal to get better. Now they were the goal for Charlie: to live long enough to see them.

What a joy-filled day when the children finally came in to meet Charlie that Wednesday! They were excited because we were, and smiles proliferated. Everyone took turns holding the dynamic duo, to Charlie's delight. His granddaughter reached out to grab his finger, the highlight of his life that day. Never was there such a proud grandpa. Twins, no less!

They managed to spend a lot of time with him and even came back after a break to see him again.

But later my phone rang while we were still at the hospital, and the telltale 207 was on the caller ID. The prison calling. Could I take any more?

I wasn't expecting the words I heard. "Charlie will be going to a nursing home. One near your home. Doesn't that make you happy? He will be given a furlough so he can go there."

Happy?

At first I was stunned with the news, and then I was ecstatic. It had been forever since I had heard such exciting news. Charlie coming home meant he would not die in the prison. Maybe the Clemency Board had heard and were merciful! And it would not be the long ride back to Warren, which would be added stress on his body.

"Oh, yes," I said, hardly daring to believe he would be near me for the end of his life. There would be no restrictions on our visits. I had been in the same nursing home after my heart surgery, and I knew they were liberal with family visits.

Charlie was more guarded in his comments about it when he heard my end of the conversation.

"I will believe it when I see it," he said.

The ensuing week was bittersweet, as my family supported Charlie and me rather than doing the planned vacationing; my daughter and her husband kept us going. At home, the grandchildren blessed me again and again with their twin antics. Each day I went to Portland to see Charlie before they even got out of bed. Then we spent the afternoons doing things. I did not come into the ICU for more than two hours so I could also visit with my family. Charlie was too tired to do much more anyway.

On Sunday, the day before my daughter was to leave, she and her husband brought the grandchildren into the hospital. Grandpa Charlie was pleased beyond description at seeing them another day. The plan was that I would come back on Monday early for a visit, after my family left for home. I had filled out papers for the nursing home previously, without much hope. Now Charlie was dying, so we fully expected him to leave and arrive at a nursing home somewhere near home at any moment. But there was also a sense of waiting for the other shoe to fall.

Chapter 31

SAYING GOOD-BYE

That afternoon, Tracey and Vincent took us to get ice cream at a local place. I was talking nonstop because of the good news about the nursing home. It was an exciting time for the twins, who were tasting their first ice cream. I had taken one of the twins to sit and wait for the treat. As the festivities continued, my phone rang and I answered, seeing the number 207 on my caller ID. Maybe it would be news of Charlie coming home to Sanford.

"Kay, I am calling you to tell you that Charlie is going back to the prison tonight after dialysis."

Why was he telling me this?

Stunned, I yelled into the phone at the man delivering such terrible news, although it was not him but probably the prison higher-ups who had made the decision. After hanging up, I explained to my daughter what was now going on. The worst of it was that with Charlie being back at the prison, I would not be able to see him like I could at the hospital or in a nursing home. The rule was only two visits of two hours per week, and those only on certain days.

But Charlie is dying, I screamed in my head. *Why do they make this so hard?* From my rarest dream to my worst nightmare in such a short time.

"Why don't you go back to the hospital now? I'll go with you if you like," Tracey said. She had no idea of the rules about this. My mind was on overload. I just could not think. I feared that Charlie would die on the way back to the prison—it was a two-hour trip and all that entailed, with the ambulance and bumps and jars along the way. At the hospital I was assured of his good care.

"Good idea. I want to see him in case he does not make it to the prison," I told Vincent and Tracey. Vincent would stay with the kids while Tracey and I went to the hospital. When Charlie had last been at the prison before this hospitalization, the prison doctor had decided that I could not visit him in the infirmary, another reason to try to see him at the hospital now. I was fairly sure he would not make it through the night and the ride. So I would take a chance that I could find a way to see him for a second visit.

On the way I explained, "We already had one visit today, and they might not let me near him. We will do what the guards say, but I am hoping they know me well enough that they will let me."

Oh, Lord, let me see him, I pleaded. I truly believed it would kill Charlie to take the trip to prison after getting his hopes up about a nursing home. But a tiny little thought crept in. God was in charge, and He was totally good. Somehow this would be good.

Finally we were at Maine Med, watching for the familiar officers from MSP. Since Charlie was going back to the prison, he would be high security again for travel. We had to get permission from them before I could go near Charlie. After one false start with an officer from MCC, I saw a familiar face. It might be my last chance to see Charlie alive.

Charlie was still at dialysis. "Could I talk to Charlie before he travels?" I asked. "I will only be a few minutes. I don't know if he can make the trip okay, and I want to say good-bye." I hoped he would see why this was so important.

"Okay, you can." *Bless him, Lord.* I could see on that MSP officer's face compassion and gravity.

Thank You, Lord. I will be able to say good-bye. He is traveling with people he knows.

I asked what direction he was likely to come from dialysis. Someone pointed, and longingly I kept my eyes focused on the elevator, looking for my beloved.

As Charlie came around the corner on a gurney, I went over and kissed him. "Do you know I have to go back to the prison?" he asked. He was absolutely furious that the prison had decided against him coming to a nursing home. "I knew they would hurt you with this."

"I will be okay, that is why I came up here. I want you to know I will be there tomorrow morning if it is at all possible, even though it is a

Monday. I will call the captain in the morning. So look for me." With rule changes, Monday was no longer a visit day. Charlie was calming down. His only worry was me.

"Hey, if I don't make it, God be with you," he said.

"You better. Good-bye, and I love you more than I can say in a lifetime."

"Me too," he said.

Charlie was indeed the love of my life, the man God had planned for me. Charlie had patiently walked with me through all the stubborn issues I had with men. He willingly took the brunt of my fury toward those in my past. Living life was so simple to him. He was able to totally embrace me, body, mind, and spirit, as no one else in my life had. I loved him, and he loved me back and offered all he had in worldly goods to me. His heart was totally mine. I could not have imagined our love, but I had spent ten years learning how sweet it was to love and be loved. As I reflected, I knew God was indeed walking this with us.

My daughter got me home for rest.

The next morning, I had a planned meeting with another local representative about the clemency bid. I said good-bye to my family as they left early to catch a plane. Then I called the prison about going in to visit Charlie on a no-visit day, since he was not going to live long. The captain said it was beyond his power to make a decision, and to call the warden a little later. But Charlie was alive. *Thank You, Lord.*

Arriving at Representative Andrea Boland's home at 7:30 in the morning, we got going on all that had happened in the last week, including Charlie's clemency bid since his life sentence was about to end. I filled her in on all that the young law student had gathered.

"Andrea, I need to call the warden while I am here at your house. I want to see Charlie each day. But the warden has to okay it because this is not a visit day. Besides, they would not let me in the infirmary the last time he was in the prison," I explained. "Could you call since she will probably not take my call?"

She called, and true to my guess, the secretary said the warden was in a meeting. She asked again who it was calling, and Andrea gave her name and title. Suddenly the warden was coming out of the meeting. Andrea explained that I was listening and wanted to talk to her, and that I was on a Bluetooth broadcast system so I could hear.

"I would like to be able to come see Charlie each day for a visit, and I know it is not a visit day. But he's dying," I said after saying hello.

"Sure, Kay. Let me get back to you. I don't know what Medical has to be doing for him."

I hung up, and Andrea and I continued our discussion of the needs for prison reform for long-timers. Faithful to her word, the warden called back at 9:30 and said I had been given permission to go each day as long as he lived. I would come that day at 1 p.m. because of the long trip ahead of me. Each visit would be the usual two hours.

My heart soared. I spent about two more minutes talking but could not concentrate, so Andrea gave special wishes to be delivered to Charlie and let me get on with my long journey. My car almost knew the way by itself over the 110 miles of roads to Charlie's side.

On arriving, I went inside. Somehow I expected the place to look different since they were going to lose their dearest prisoner soon. But it did not. Security functions on sameness, day after day after day sameness. Then I said to a surprised lobby guard, "I am here to see Charlie, and I have permission from the warden to see him at Medical." Understandably, the front desk officer called the warden's office to confirm what I had just said. Conditioned to sameness, their defense goes up when a different situation arises.

The escort people had not been notified of my visit, so I had to wait, but that was a small price. For all the problems I had encountered along the way, I have to say Maine State Prison was at their finest in allowing me permission to come see Charlie each day until he died. He had survived the ambulance ride. But there was more to come.

Knowing that I could come see him each day, Charlie was very happy. It was my last gift to him. There were a few others in the infirmary, and they were friendly men. The officers were kind, knowing the outcome for us.

Each moment of each day was precious, and we were joyful together no matter what happened. News from Tracey arriving back at her home was good. I was allowed to read cards from other inmates who had written him through me at home. They kindly let the cards in. I could help Charlie eat what he could eat. He liked me reading Scripture to him. And still he talked of getting better and going back to work.

"Why don't you look through my bags and find my wedding ring?" he asked the first morning. "It's in my denture case." Charlie had not been able to wear his ring because it kept falling off long before the final amputation in February. One hundred and fifty pounds had dropped off his body along the way somewhere.

"I would love to wear it on my chain," I smiled "Where is it?"

"In those bags over there, inside my denture box. It is in a little blue box," he said, indicating with his frail finger the clear trash bags stuffed in the shower of the infirmary cell. He had told me months before that he kept the ring in that box where no one would think to look for it. Being sick, he was unable to keep watch on his belongings very well. "We will get Property to okay the release of the ring to you."

I went right over and took out a bag to look. The bag clunked on the floor, so I knew an officer would appear, wondering what we were doing. Caught red-handed with the bag, I looked up.

"What was that? What are you doing?" the officer asked. He did not look gruff. Just keeping track of us while giving us some privacy.

"I am trying to find Charlie's denture case." I was not going to reveal that it was the hiding place of his ring to anyone.

"She's looking for my wedding ring," Charlie spoke emphatically. "It is in my denture case." I figured Charlie knew more about who could know what and when. So I showed the guard the bag.

This kind officer came over and started looking with me through the first bag and then the other bags, asking Charlie more questions about the ring as time went along. We could not see the blue denture cup in any of the bags. Finally the officer said he would get hold of Property and see if they had it.

"Something valuable like that should be in Property," he assured Charlie.

Every day after that I asked the officer, when I came in, if they had found the ring. I knew Charlie was dying and wanted me to wear his ring on my chain for him. They had called Property, but no one had any idea where it was.

Charlie instructed me to make sure I took everything when he died. "I want you to have it all. Don't leave anything."

Each day was precious, the two hours together to talk or just soothe his pain as best I could. Precious love was spoken between us. Our life together had always been measured by the beginning and end of a visit. These few hours a day were filled with speaking every word of love and laughter we could remember to say because we had been trained by the Lord in what was important in the time we had. Oh, how beautifully the Lord had prepared us for this last task!

All spring long, I had been praying a line I'd heard in a song: "Lord, will I have time to say good-bye?" The Lord had been preparing us for this time. Perhaps our most desperate plea to the Lord was that Charlie would die with me by his side. That was our simple desire. And that we would be alone. I wanted so desperately to be with him, but chances of him dying during my two-hour visits were slim. *Lord, what can You do about this?*

On July 26 I went in to find Charlie in a lot more pain than he could stand. I could hear him as soon as I went through the door to the infirmary. Nurses were giving him morphine when I arrived. Finally allowed to go in after his care, I did not even get a greeting. He just weakly uttered, "Help me with the pain." I knew several things that had worked in the past few days, and I tried each one, talking with a soothing voice. I could massage his back, and that seemed to help. He had told me one time that my voice was not too bad, so I sang choruses of worship. I was allowed into a bathroom near his cell to wet a washcloth for his forehead. All stops were out. With all the lists of "no" finally vacated by the staff, I was allowed to do whatever I could to comfort him, but the clock was ticking very near our two-hour limit.

I knew. Charlie would not live until the next day. They were giving him so much medication, and he was not refusing it. Getting close to the time I would have to leave, I asked the officer on duty if he could get permission for me to stay until Charlie died. Immediately he said yes, and lots of people started to come to say good-bye. Graciously, the warden okayed my stay past the two allotted hours.

One last funny story that would help us now at this difficult hour: At MSP, a reveille call goes over the intercom signaling count. For the inmates, that means back to lockup. I knew this because in 2009 in the hospital one time, an officer played reveille on his phone recorder while Charlie was sleeping. Charlie woke immediately. "What is that?" he asked, confused. Years of rising when the call was broadcast made him start. Back then, I noticed the officer holding up his smartphone with a grin.

"Charlie, he is pulling your leg. He played that from his phone."

Charlie had been in prison nearly thirty years at the time, and he had never seen a cell phone in the prison except what he could envision from TV. There was no way he could know all a smartphone would do.

I explained, "Charlie, cell phones do a lot of things, and he recorded the bugle call is my guess."

With a huge laugh the officer gave himself away, and once again we had a good belly laugh with Charlie. Then Charlie explained to me that count was signaled each day, each time with reveille. I had been in the infirmary during a few lockups and had to leave his cell and go out to the corridor to wait it out, praying it would not last long so I could go back to see Charlie. But I had never been through a count.

Now, here on his last day, reveille came over the intercom a while after the time was up for a regular two-hour visit. Charlie, faithful to his training, wanted me to go. He could hardly raise his hand, but he wanted me to get out of there so I would not get in trouble. With every bit of his last strength he raised his hand, trying to protect me.

"Charlie, it is okay for me to be here. They gave me special permission. You are not going to make it much longer."

Obviously in a great deal of pain and confusion, he asked me several times, "Dear, what am I going to do? I'm so tired." He reached for my hand. I was so grateful to be able to touch him, rub his back, and put more cloths on his forehead.

"Charlie, you are going to see the face of Jesus soon, and He will reach out His hand to you. Take it. No more pain. No more locks and keys. *You're getting out of prison today. And you are going to a feast with our King.* I love you so much, Sweetheart. Go to sleep."

"Yup. I am so tired. Love you, Honey." And he fell asleep.

People were in and out, but finally they left us alone, and I stayed praying and reading Scripture until my dear Charlie breathed his last breath. I knew he was being swept up into the arms of our loving Jesus, the One who had brought us together in the first place. To paraphrase the great Dr. King, "Free at last. Free at last. Thank God almighty, he was free at last."

Chapter 32
REFLECTIONS

S aying good-bye to Charlie opened a new chapter in my life. Devastated by the immensity of the loss, at first I could only think, *Lord?* I could not even figure out how to start my life without Charlie other than call family and friends on the way home from the prison.

Literally all my friends helped in some way. My children mobilized to get there for the memorial service with all their children. From Canada, upstate New York, North Carolina, and Connecticut they came. Several spoke at the memorial. River of Life mobilized their love for me to attend to my every need. Friends helped in countless ways. St. George's Episcopal Church lovingly provided a larger building to hold the service, along with helping a great deal with the costs. And hundreds of people attended Charlie's memorial. The service went on for two hours *after* what we had planned so everyone could speak of this wonderful man and our breathtaking God.

Over and over through my years with Charlie and right up until he died, all my children managed to love Charlie, each in their own way. They saw his love for me and wanted it for me enough to overcome their personal reluctance to accept him and to move forward in spite of their stereotypes about prisoners. Some met him and some did not, but they all came with their families to the memorial service.

My children and their spouses are a constant blessing and surprise. My son Gage wrote the day after Charlie's memorial service, "I am glad we decided to come to the tribute to Charlie. I am so sorry we never got to meet him in person, but Jessica, myself, and the kids really felt like we got to know him on Saturday. I was one of those people, like Kenny and Ray, who thought when you first announced you were marrying a guy from prison that you were 'crazy.'"

In Kona, Hawaii, I received a prophetic word from a teacher on the YWAM mission base saying that the Lord would restore *all* that the locusts had taken. Devastated by the crash of my life both before and after divorce, my first tiny thought was that maybe God would give me a person who would be perfect for me as well as me being perfect for him. After all, He had already given me children, a dream job, and a family around the world.

That word came ten years before I ever wrote Charlie the first letter. Over those years I prayed on and off for the unknown man God had chosen—for his peace, for his journey with the Lord, for his well-being, and for us to find our way to each other. It appears the Lord moved heaven and earth to bring us together. When I finally trusted Charlie enough to even consider that I was in love, I knew suddenly that he was the answer to that prayer over the years. Many men had been around me or in my thoughts, but it had never occurred to me before 2002 that my man would live inside the walls.

There was nothing I could not share and trust to my beloved mate. And he grabbed hold of abandon and trust with me. I had finally shouted inside my being, *Lord, I will do whatever is in my power to make our marriage work, because I know this man is a treasure for me, a perfect choice.*

On this path, I learned a good deal about those who are imprisoned. We who live in the United States are five percent of the world population, and yet we incarcerate twenty-five percent of the prisoners on earth. According to the Pew report "One in 31: The Long Reach of American Corrections," one in thirty-one people are currently in jail or prison or on probation or parole. That does not include those who were released yesterday or those who will be released tomorrow. One in thirty-one. What is wrong with that picture? And we are called to be a voice for the voiceless anywhere we meet them. In my experience, there are some inside who probably are not going to change, but we do not know who and should be expecting that a correctional system will be correcting many. God certainly changed Charlie.

When I talk to people about prisons and prisoners, the first things I tell them are that Charlie's crime was murder and that we did not have conjugal rights. That is what people usually want to know and will not ask. Then I challenge them with "raise your hand" questions. "Do you believe that God can change people? Do you believe that He can change someone in prison? And further, do you believe He can change someone who committed murder?" My heart now sings because I found in God the love we desire, and this love came through a man who happened to be inside the walls.

Before I met Charlie, I too had bought into the world's way of resolving all manner of crime in the US: long sentences and lock 'em up and forget them. Out of sight, out of mind. No second chances. But people in prison are first of all people. All of us have committed a crime and fallen short of the mark. (Did you ever go over the speed limit?) We are called to speak for the voiceless, and somehow we must tackle the challenge of prisons in the United States. Our prison system remains one of the most disagreeable marks on us as a people. Will we be part of the problem or part of the solution?

God in His wisdom gave me His best in this man. Do I miss Charlie? Deeply. Will I see him again? Yes. In the end of our journey on earth together, I stood facing the world outside, knowing that God had changed me. Charlie's and my world was better, more intimate because we did our time together well. But I know our God has unending joys and sorrows for me as I go forward into the unknown. In the pain, in the risk, and in the passion, I am desperate for Him who has pursued me. And I set my eyes forward.

Like Dr. King said, I have a dream. As the months of grieving pass, I am saddened by how many of us miss what God has for us by excluding and marginalizing a whole population of men and women based on a past sin. Rather than fear, can we embrace prisoners and ex-prisoners with loving arms instead?

See! The winter is past;
the rains are over and gone.
Flowers appear on the earth;
the season of singing has come,
the cooing of doves
is heard in our land.
(Song of Solomon 2:11–12, NIV)

Contact the author:
kaydoingtime@yahoo.com
Website:
doingtimewithcharlie.org